Soldier's Wife

Cotton Fields to Berlin and Tripoli

Rickey Butch Walker

March 2016

Published by:

Bluewater Publications
1812 CR 111
Killen, Alabama 35645
www.BluewaterPublications.com

Bluewater Publications
books by
Rickey Butch Walker

Appalachian Indians of the Warrior Mountains: History and Culture, ISBN 978-1-934610-72-5, $14.95

Appalachian Indian Trails of the Chickamauga: Lower Cherokee Settlements, ISBN 978-1-934610-91-6, $14.95

Celtic Indian Boy of Appalachia: A Scots Irish Cherokee Childhood, ISBN 978-1-934610-75-6, $14.95

Chickasaw Chief George Colbert: His Family and His Country, ISBN 978-1-934610-71-8, $19.95

Doublehead: Last Chickamauga Cherokee Chief, ISBN 978-1-934610-67-1, $19.95

Hiking Sipsey: A Family's Fight for Eastern Wilderness, ISBN 978-1-934610-93-0, $14.95

Soldier's Wife: Cotton Fields to Berlin and Tripoli, ISBN 978-1-934610-12-1, $14.95

Warrior Mountains Folklore: American Indian and Celtic History in the Southeast, ISBN 978-1-934610-65-7, $24.95

Warrior Mountains Indian Heritage-Teacher's Edition, ISBN 978-1-934610-27-5, $39.95

Warrior Mountains Indian Heritage-Student Edition, ISBN 978-1-934610-66-4, $24.95

Works in Progress

Cotton was King: Indians to Slave Plantations

Black Folk Tales of Appalachia: Slavery to Survival

Acknowledgements

This book is based primarily on interviews with my paternal Aunt Katie Lucille (Lucy) Walker, and it is as accurate as her memory allowed. I interviewed her several times over the course of some two years. She was excited and proud that I was doing a book about her years as a military wife. She talked to me on days that I know that she was not feeling her best. One day while doing home dialysis, she told me stories with a smile on her face. She was a very special aunt that I highly respected and admired. I thank my Aunt Katie Lucille (Lucy) Walker for sharing the story of her life as a soldier's wife.

Martha Jo Walker Wise, the oldest daughter of my Aunt Lucille, provided pictures and stories of her family. Martha Jo was extremely helpful in completing this book about her mother. Without her help, this book would not have been possible. Thank you Martha Jo for all you did to help me. A special thank you is given to all of Aunt Lucille's children, family members, and friends who contributed information used in this book.

I also thank my sisters Dianne Walker Thrasher and June Walker Reed for their assistance with photographs, text suggestions, and editing the manuscript. Since both of my sisters are older than Aunt Lucille's children and I, they were able to share stories about her that otherwise would not have been told.

The editor of this book, June Walker Reed, spent countless hours making corrections to the text. I do not have the words to express my deepest gratitude to June for her help. Without her expertise, the quality of this book would be greatly diminished. I thank you, June, for your dedication to the completion of this book.

Table of Contents

Soldier's Wife

Cotton Fields to Berlin and Tripoli

Introduction

This is a true story about the challenges faced by a poverty stricken country girl who was born during the Great Depression and grew up in a sparsely populated rural farming community during World War II. The narrative as given by Katie Lucille Walker is about her early life, her family members, events she recalled, and her journey around the globe following her soldier. Her story touches on moments in history that helped shape her life and the lives of her children as she traveled from the cotton fields of North Alabama to the war torn chaos of Berlin, Germany, and Tripoli, Libya.

Katie Lucille talked about growing up in poverty when getting by was just that. She went from a mischievous school girl wearing her brother's hand me down plow boots and homemade print dresses made from flour sacks to a sophisticated young woman dressed in the latest fashions. She had never shopped in a major department store nor eaten in a fancy restaurant until after she married her soldier at the age of eighteen. She was strong southern woman who was just as comfortable eating a biscuit out of a tin syrup bucket as she was eating a steak from a fine China plate.

One would never dream that a poor country girl from the cotton patches of North Alabama would see the world during the 1950's and 1960's, but it happened. On April 18, 1952, Katie Lucille (Lucy) Walker left the cotton fields of North Alabama to travel to some of the most turbulent war torn places the world has ever known. For some eighteen years, she followed her career military husband around the world.

1

Katie Lucille left the south land of generations of her ancestors to be with her true love Asa (Ace) Francis Walker, Jr. as he served in the United States Air Force. During the chaotic aftermath of World War II, Asa and Lucy were assigned to politically unstable places at the height of the Cold War. Katie Lucille made sacrifices of home, parents, siblings, and friends to see that her husband could have his family by his side no matter where he was stationed around the world.

Katie Lucille Walker
Berlin Germany 1961

Katie Lucille (Lucy) Walker's remarkable journey was similar to that experienced by many other military wives as they tried to maintain a semblance of family while continually on the move supporting their husbands who were serving in the armed forces in order that our country might be free. The price of freedom did not come cheap. Lucy gave birth and reared five children, in addition to losing two babies, while on the move to countries that were immersed in political turmoil such as Berlin, Germany, and Tripoli, Libya. These moves were not without sacrifice of being away from home and loved

2

ones. It was something she did without complaint. She sacrificed in order to honor the wishes of her husband and to keep their family united. She knew there would be challenges for being a soldier's wife.

Asa and Katie Lucille Walker traveled the world from the early 1950's though September of 1970 as a military family serving in the United States Air Force. Their three older children were reared far away from the hill country homes of Lucy's North Alabama ancestors. Her parents were poor subsistence cotton farmers who used mules to plant their crops. Katie Lucille was the youngest of fourteen children of Monroe Daniel (Dan) Walker and Maudy Nevady (Vady) Legg Walker.

Katie Lucille and her mother developed a tight bond. Their relationship was one that only a mother and baby daughter could share. She did not find out for days about the passing of her mother. The Red Cross and the military were unable to get her the message of the death of her beloved mother. No amount of tears and heartache could ease her pain or would allow Katie Lucille a last chance to see her mother.

Lucy harbored a lifetime of hurt feelings over her mother's death because she did not attend the funeral. It had been several months since Katie Lucille had gotten to go home for a visit with her mother and daddy. This made the death seem much more painful to a daughter who loved her mother beyond words. Such were the sacrifices that a country girl from North Alabama had to make in the service of our great country and loyalty to her career military husband.

Her survival in faraway lands was not always easy because the military wages were barely enough to get by and certainly not enough to provide a life of luxury. She had to take care of her family the best way she could in places foreign to her humble birth. Loyalty to her husband and children was an inherent trait that had been passed down through generations of her mixed Celtic Indian families that eked out a living on the poor mountainous soils of North Alabama.

Katie Lucille (Lucy) Walker and Asa Francis Walker, Jr.'s family moved in all sorts of situations and even in the middle of the night. These moves were solely Lucy's responsibility because the military did not consider the enlisted man's family its responsibility. Sometimes Katie Lucille was given no reason for the move, but as a soldier's wife, she responded without question or hesitation.

She had no idea where their next home would be nor what type of living conditions they would have to endure. Service to the United States was a duty that she accepted. Asa knew that the military would be his life, and Lucy was not about to leave his side.

Asa Walker
Berlin Germany 1961

Even though Asa was serving with the security service in the United States Air Force, both he and Lucy were determined to keep their family together against all odds. They usually lived no more than a year at a time in one place in a foreign country. This military family was ready, willing, and able to move on a very short notice.

One such move was a daring middle of the night escape when there was the threat that enemy military forces were about to take the entire town where Lucy's family lived. Katie Lucille witnessed some terrible incidents of the Cold War. From her upstairs window, she had seen innocent men, women, and children being gunned down. Many people seeking freedom were shot to death at the hands of enemy soldiers guarding the area.

One particular night while her husband was on duty, Katie Lucille was with her sleeping children along with other security service families who were being housed together for military protection; a loud knock came on the door. She and others were told by United States soldiers to get their children and get out now. Lucy grabbed a few clothes and dressed herself and her children. She was allowed to take one suitcase. She had to leave all personal belongings behind. They immediately boarded the military transport waiting to carry the families to the airport.

On a moment's notice, Katie Lucille, who was expecting a baby, and her three young children were on a military plane in the late hours of the night flying to an unknown destination. Earlier, Lucy had witnessed a young girl the age of her daughter getting shot and killed. She was afraid of what might happen to her children, but she never allowed them to see her fear. Survival of her family dictated her response. At dawn the next morning, Katie Lucille and her children landed in a new country.

She had no idea of the fate of her husband who was serving with the security service. At that time, cell phones were unheard of. With a strong determination and strength, Aunt Lucille said, "Cell phones are just damnation, they cause divorces. I do not even want one." Survival to her was not directed by a friendly phone call. There was no way that she could know what was happening to her husband or his unit. Such were the struggles that Katie Lucille Walker faced for her children, husband, family, and homeland.

On one occasion, Katie Lucille made a daring escape from the jaws of death clad only in a hospital gown and baby diapers. After being induced, Lucy was handed her new born baby boy, and the Muslim hospital staff fled for their lives. Katie Lucille and another young black American female who had just been forced to give birth had to find a way to survive. Attempting to escape in the middle of a war was a life and death struggle.

Katie Lucille Walker was caught in the chaos where American military men were being shot and killed, but she never showed fear. Survival for her family and not fear dictated her actions. In the midst of the gun battles going on around her, Katie Lucille led her comrade into the streets that were filled with the terrifying sights and sounds of war. War or peace, she would always be a soldier's wife.

After Asa's retirement, Lucy and Asa moved within sight of her old home place in present-day Morgan County, Alabama. Asa and Katie Lucille Walker resided at their final home which was located about a mile northwest from where Lucy spent the majority of her early childhood.

Katie Lucille held various jobs while following her military husband around the world. After returning home to Alabama, Lucy continued to work and launched her own sales career. She was very successful as a business woman of some twenty six years. However, from the day she married a military man, Katie Lucille (Lucy) Walker was honored and proud to be called a soldier's wife.

Now, begins her life's journey from the cotton patches to Berlin and Tripoli. Her remarkable story of the years she and her children followed her military husband on his tours of duty unfolds in the pages of this book, "Soldier's Wife."

Chapter One

Katie Lucille (Lucy) Walker's Family

"Katie Lucille Walker was my birth name, but when I got married I dropped the name Katie. I do not care if you call me Katie in the book," stated my Aunt Lucille. Katie was a family name that came from Catherine Kingfisher a full blood Cherokee whose nickname was spelled Katy or Katie. Katie Kingfisher married John Walker, a half blood Cherokee. John Walker was Katie Lucille's fourth great grandfather.

When Katie Lucille Walker was born on May 26, 1933, the country was in the depths of the Great Depression which lasted from 1929 until 1939. In January 1933, Franklin Delano Roosevelt took office of President of the United States. He initiated numerous government relief programs in an effort to pull the country out of the Great Depression.

Katie Lucille said, "I was born in the middle of the great depression, and we were very poor." Her large family of twelve was just trying to survive. The primary concern of her parents was having food to eat, a roof over their head, and clothes to wear. Although times were hard, they like many of the poor farming families of North Alabama had been struggling to make ends meet long before the Great Depression, and they would continue to do so for years following the depression.

There was hardly any industry in the hill country of Appalachia including Winston and Lawrence Counties of North Alabama where Katie Lucille's family made their home, and few people had jobs away from the farm even before the depression. Unemployment was rampant. Finding work was extremely difficult because most people had no money to hire employees. In spite of all the government relief programs, living conditions were extremely harsh to say the least. It was under these adverse conditions that Dan and Vady Walker delivered their youngest child into the world.

For the first few years of Katie Lucille's life, living conditions were very difficult for her family, but as Hank Williams, Jr. sang, *"Country folks can survive.*" Although survival was difficult, they managed to eke out an existence on the poor hillsides. Katie said, "I was born on May 26, 1933, in a one room log cabin just inside the east edge of Lawrence County," Alabama. "At the time of my birth, all twelve of us lived in that old log cabin. The house did not have a fire place and was just one big room. The log cabin was located on county road 200; it was up on a hill."

The family's economic situation did not improve greatly until Katie Lucille got old enough to marry and move away from home. After the Walker family moved, the log cabin was abandoned, but it remained pretty much intact for the next eighty years. She remembered, "The old cabin was taken down about four years ago. I wanted wood from the old home, but Mr. Hill would not agree to that."

It was not uncommon for poor southern farmers, many of whom had Indian ancestry, to live in small log cabins. Lucy's mixed blood Cherokee Scots Irish family had migrated through North Carolina to Tennessee then to Georgia into Alabama and west all the way into Oklahoma and Texas. Many of Lucy's ancestors were of American Indian descent. Katie Lucille Walker said, "We were told by my daddy that the Indian lady in the history books was like his grandma who was (American) Indian, but daddy never talked a lot about us being Indian."

At that time, it was not popular to discuss one's Indian heritage. Many old folks had a fear of being sent west to Indian Territory. It was quite common for people to deny their American Indian heritage for fear of discrimination. In fact, it was illegal to be American Indian in Alabama until after the 1968 Civil Rights Act was passed by the United States Congress. Specifically, sections two through seven of the Civil Rights Act allowed mixed blood Indian people in the southeast to be enumerated American Indian.

The grandparents of Katie Lucille Walker were Sidney Walker and Louisa Vicey Stevens, the parents of Dan Walker. Vicey, who was born in October 1854, was the daughter of an Indian woman by the name of Elizabeth Buzbee. In her later years, Vicey lived with her son Dan until her death in 1938. At that time Katie Lucille was only five years old, and she recalled little about her grandmother. However, Katie Lucille's brother Brady Walker remembered his Grandma Vicey very well.

Brady Walker told his children, "Grandma was an Indian lady who loved to smoke her corncob pipe and chew tobacco." Brady was thirteen years old when his grandmother died at the Dan Walker home place on Highway 41 in Morgan County, Alabama. According to Brady, "When Grandma Vicey died, dad was away from home, and the neighbors did not attend the wake because grandma was an Indian."

As cultural diversity became more acceptable, Lucy's family members acknowledged their American Indian heritage and visited with their Indian relatives in Oklahoma. Indian relatives from Texas and Oklahoma visited the Walker family in Alabama. Lucy's relatives including her brother Brady and other family members attended the funerals of his dad's sisters who live along the Red River separating part of Texas and Oklahoma. They learned a great deal more regarding their Native ancestors.

Brady and Novel Walker near Idabell, Oklahoma
Red River Bridge to Texas 7/3/1978

Most of Katie Lucille's aunts and uncles lived along the Red River in Oklahoma and Texas. In addition to Katie Lucille's father, Monroe Daniel (Dan) Walker, Sidney and Louisa Vicey had six other children: Mary Ann, Louisa, James C., William A., Sarah Elizabeth, and Lucinda. After Sidney's death, Vicey and her children moved to the Red River area of either Oklahoma or Texas.

According to Calvin Walker, his father William A. (Will) moved back to Alabama around 1915. Calvin's older brother Doyle Benton Walker was born in Texas on May 9, 1913, and Calvin was born in Alabama on June 8, 1916. Will

9

Walker was the uncle of Katie Lucille. Her father Dan had moved back to Alabama from Texas before the time of his marriage in 1907.

Years later, another uncle of Katie Lucille's, James Columbus Walker moved from Oklahoma to Alabama, and he lived with Dan and Vady for a considerable period of time. James was born December 22, 1872, and he died September 26, 1960. He was known by all family members as "Uncle Jemes." Uncle Jemes had Indian features; he had a very dark complexion, high cheekbones, straight black hair, and extremely dark eyes.

As a young boy, I was afraid of Uncle Jemes because he was different looking and much darker than my other lighter complexion folks. He always carried silver dollars in his overall pockets. Frequently, I could hear him making a noise by flipping those silver dollars between his fingers inside his pockets. Although I was only eleven years old when Uncle Jemes died, I will never forget the jingle of those silver coins flipping together.

Some of the Walker children showed their Indian blood.
Brady, Dan, Vady, Oliver, Ida, Lodean, Paul, Roy

Katie's Ancestors

Katie Lucille's ancestors and kinfolks were scattered across the southern portion of the United States. Her people lived and were buried from Georgia all the way to the Red River area of Texas and Oklahoma. Katie Lucille Walker's direct line was John Walker and Catherine (Katie) Kingfisher, who had a son named William Walker I. The family name William was usually passed down to the eldest son. William I was born in 1762, and he was Lucy's great, great, great grandfather. William I had a son named William II who was born in 1792. William II had a son William III who was born in 1820. William III had a son in 1856 named Sidney, who named his first son William. Sidney's youngest son

11

Dan Walker who was Katie Lucille's father was born in 1888. Dan continued and an old family tradition by naming his first born son William Roy Walker.

Katie Lucille's great grandfather William Walker III was born on March 15, 1820, in Cocke County, Tennessee. William III who married Mary A. Vaughn lived in Georgia before moving to Morgan County, Alabama. Katie Lucille's great grandmother Mary A. Vaughn was born in South Carolina in 1831 and died March 19, 1871, in Winston County, Alabama. She was buried in the Warrior Mountains at Old Houston Cemetery on the east side of Brushy Creek in Winston County. From the marriage of William and Mary came the birth of Lucy's grandfather Sidney A. Walker on December 31, 1856, in Polk County, Georgia.

Prior to the age of forty-five, William III enlisted for a three year term with the Union Army at Camp Davis, Mississippi, on December 14, 1863. He served as a member of the First Alabama Cavalry, Company I, and he fought for the Union during the Civil War. He was discharged July 19, 1865. On August 12, 1867, William III signed the Loyalty Oath to the Union in Winston County, Alabama, along with his father William II and his brother Jonathan, as reported by the 1867 Voting Registration and Loyalty Oath.

Just two months after the death of his wife Mary A. Vaughn, William III married Elizabeth Nelson of Morgan County on May 8, 1871. At the time of his mother's death and the remarriage of his father, Sidney Walker was only fourteen years old. Therefore, Sidney probably moved to Mississippi with his father and step mother.

William III and Elizabeth moved to Yalobusha County, Mississippi, where they had several other children. William Walker III died in December 1886, and he was buried in the Walker-Big Spring Cemetery in Yalobusha County, Mississippi, just a few miles south of present-day Highway 278. Some of their children were buried near their parents in the Walker Cemetery in Mississippi.

Lucy's grandfather Sidney, son of William III and his first wife Mary A. Vaughn, married Louisa Vicey Stevens on January 14, 1875, in Blount County, Alabama. Probate Judge J. W. Moon performed their wedding ceremony which took place near the burial site of Sidney's great grandfather William Walker I, who was buried at Old Nectar Cemetery in Blount County. For a short time following their wedding, Sidney and Vicey lived in Blount County near Old Nectar.

By February 1876, Sidney and Vicey were living in Marion County, Alabama, and they lived there until after the United States Census of June 4, 1880. Since Marion County, Alabama, is adjacent to Mississippi, Sidney and Vicey may have been living in proximity to his father William III and his stepmother Elizabeth. Also, Sidney is found in the 1880 census of Hill County, Texas, and he was listed as a boarder. According to family history, Sidney was said to be on the run from law enforcement authorities.

By the time of the birth of Sidney and Vicey's son William A. (Will) on February 25, 1884, the family was again living in Marion County, Alabama. Prior to the birth of Lucy's father Monroe Daniel (Dan) on June 18, 1888, Sidney and Vicey were living near Cedar Town in Polk County, Georgia. Apparently, they had moved back to Sidney's childhood home. Two years later in February 1890, they were living in Winston County, Alabama, where their youngest daughter Lucinda was born. Shortly after her birth, Sidney was shot.

Lucy's oldest brother William Roy Walker related a story that he was told when he was a young boy. His grandfather Sidney was preparing for a hunting trip. Sidney was leaning on his rabbit eared shotgun when a big hound jumped up for a pat on the head. When the dog went back to the ground, his foot caught on one of the hammers and discharged the gun. The pellets of the shotgun entered Sidney's stomach. As a result of the injury, he suffered three days before he died.

Other members of Katie Lucille's family claimed that Sidney was staying on the move to prevent being caught by authorities, and the shooting may have occurred during the commission of a bank or train robbery. It was reported that in 1880, Sidney was in Texas on the run from the law. Some even speculated that Sidney rode with the famous Jesse James, prior to the gunfighter's death on April 3, 1882. Still others speculated that Sidney was making moonshine whiskey, and he may have been shot by federal revenuers while they were raiding his illegal operation. No one will ever know for sure because the older generations took that information to the grave.

Regardless of the cause of his death, Sidney died on September 20, 1890, after being shot in the stomach which was claimed to be a hunting accident. At the time of the shooting, he was supposedly at Brown's Spring near Looney's Tavern in Winston County, Alabama. The tavern was located adjacent to the Indian trail that became known as the Old Jasper Road or present-day Alabama Highway 41.

Brady and Novel Walker in Texas
Red River Bridge to Oklahoma 7/2/1978

Sidney's wife and the children were listed on the Cullman County Census in 1900; however, shortly after Sidney was killed, family lore stated that Vicey and her children moved to Texas. It is well documented that several of her grandchildren were born along the Red River that runs between Texas and Oklahoma. Many of Sidney and Vicey's children and grandchildren remained in the west all their lives. During her lifetime, Katie Lucille recalled that many of the older cousins from Texas and Oklahoma would come to Alabama for a visit with their uncle Dan Walker. These western kinfolks would spend several days visiting their relatives in Alabama.

Sidney was buried next to his grandfather William II, who was born on December 25, 1792, and died about 1900. William II and his grandson Sidney were buried in Old Emeus Cemetery at Logan in Cullman County, Alabama. The cemetery at Logan was adjacent to an Indian trail known as Black Warriors' Path. William II's father was William I, who was also buried next to the same Indian trail in the Old Nectar Cemetery in Blount County, Alabama.

14

The Black Warriors' Path ran from present-day St. Augustine, Florida, to Nashville, Tennessee. Several generations of Katie Lucille's older ancestors gradually migrated northward along the old Indian trail where they lived, died, and were buried. Her early family members migrated from Blount County to Cullman County then Winston County and eventually into Lawrence County, Alabama. Some of her folks were buried in Old Nectar Cemetery, Old Emeus Cemetery, and at Oakville Indian Mound Cemetery all of which are adjacent to the Black Warriors' Path.

Lucy's great, great, great grandfather William I was born about 1762 and died on July 3, 1841. He was three fourths Cherokee Indian. William I was the son of Catherine Kingfisher and John Walker as stated in Doctor Emmet McDonald Starr's 1921 book *"History of the Cherokees."* William I and his brother or half-brother Tandy Walker II (1760-1841) were buried at Old Nectar near the Black Warriors' Path.

While living in the Creek Indian territory of the Warrior River drainage in 1812, Tandy Walker II helped secure the release of Martha Crawley. She was taken captive at the Duck River crossing of the Natchez Trace and became a prisoner of the Creek Indians. The Martha Crawley incident is historically recorded.

William I and Tandy II were Indian traders and scouts. It has been reported that in October 1813, Tandy and William Walker warned the Creek Indians living at Black Warriors' Town that they were going to be attacked by General Andrew Jackson's forces during the Creek Indian War. When Jackson's army arrived, Black Warriors' Town had just been abandoned.

Author Butch Walker at grave of Tandy W. Walker, McDonald Cemetery on Coosa Path, also called the Muscle Shoals Path just east of Pathkiller Creek. He was an Alabama legislator 1838 - 1843 and son of Tandy Walker II, Indian trader and scout.

Tandy II's son Tandy Walker III was buried on the Indian trail known as the Coosa Path in the McDonald Cemetery in Moulton, Alabama. Tandy III's wife Elizabeth was buried near the Black Warriors' Path on the Copena Indian Burial Mound Cemetery at Oakville Indian Mounds Park in Lawrence County, Alabama. Elizabeth's sister-in-law Sarah Walker Hodges, daughter of Tandy Walker II and wife of William Hodges, was also buried on top of the mound.

The same Black Warriors' Path that ran past the old log house at Corinth in Cullman County were Lucy's parents were married continued beyond the Oakville Indian Mounds Park in Lawrence County, Alabama. Along the park's western boundary, the Indian path passed by the west edge of the Oakville Ceremonial Mound and within a few yards west of the Copena Burial Mound and Cemetery. Although Katie Lucille's ancestral family was scattered over the southeastern United States, many of her direct line ancestors found their final resting places in close proximity to her childhood home on Highway 41 in Morgan County, Alabama.

Dan Walker and Vady Legg Walker

Katie Lucille (Lucy) Walker said, "My daddy was Monroe Daniel Walker and my mother was Maudy Nevady Legg." Lucy's father was called Dan Walker, and he was born in Polk County, Georgia, on June 18, 1888. For a number of years, Dan Walker's parents had moved back and forth from Polk County, Georgia, to Winston County, Alabama.

Many of Katie Lucille (Lucy) Walker's early ancestors lived, died, and were buried along the old Indian trails that crisscrossed North Alabama. Her parents were married at the junction of two Indian trails. The High Town Path and the Black Warriors' Path intersected near the house where Lucy's parents Monroe Daniel (Dan) Walker and Maudy Nevady (Vady) Legg were married. The wedding took place on January 31, 1907, at Corinth Community near the crossing of these two Indian trails. J. W. Bryant, Justice of the Peace, preformed the wedding ceremony at the home of Vady's parents Addison Laten Legg and Fertemie Elizabeth Speakman Legg.

16

Addison and Elizabeth Legg lived in a big old log house that stood in the Corinth Community on the northwest edge of Cullman County. Located near the corners of Morgan, Cullman, Winston, and Lawrence Counties, Corinth was a small community at the junction of these two old Indian trails. The High Town Path, an east to west Indian trail that ran along the Tennessee Divide of northwest Alabama, later became known as the Old Corn Road. The Black Warriors' Path ran north to slightly northwest to southeast. From Piney Grove just west of Corinth, the two old Indian trails merged with another Indian trail known as the Old Jasper Road. All three trails continued to Cave Springs Cemetery where the trails divided with the High Town Path and Black Warriors' Path following the Tennessee Divide west and the old Jasper Road continuing to the north.

Dan and Vady

After they were married, Dan and Vady made their home south of Upshaw between Boone Creek and Indian Creek in Winston County. Prior to Lucy's birth, they moved to the east edge of Lawrence County just a few miles north of Piney Grove. When Lucy was just a little girl, the Walker family moved to a farm that was located on the Old Jasper Road which is present-day Alabama Highway 41 in Morgan County. Dan and Vady settled within a ten mile radius of Vady's childhood home. They bought a farm, cleared the land, and built their house. They lived there until their deaths almost thirty years later not far from the log house on the High Town Path where they were married some sixty years earlier.

Maudy Nevady Legg was born on August 28, 1891. According to Katie Lucille, "My mama was born west of Hartselle in Morgan County, Alabama. She was the daughter of Addison Legg, and her mother was Elizabeth Speakman before she married. Grandpa Addison Legg's people all lived there."

Lucy's maternal uncles and other members of the Legg family lived in Cullman, Morgan, and Winston Counties. Lucy's ancestors on her mother's side of the family built the Legg Covered Bridge across Crooked Creek in Cullman County, Alabama. Originally the bridge was known as the Legg Covered Bridge, but after the construction of the Clarkson's Grist Mill, the bridge was renamed. Today, it is known as the Clarkson-Legg Bridge; descendants of the Legg family still live in the area.

Katie Lucille was seven years old when her grandmother Fertemie Elizabeth Speakman Legg died. After the death of Elizabeth on February 8, 1940, Addison married for a second time. Aunt Lucille said, "Before Grandpa Legg died with cancer, he married Lucinda (Aunt Cindy) Wilbanks," who was born on October 3, 1881. Lucinda was thirteen years younger than Addison, who was born on December 26, 1868. Lucinda was barely four years older than Addison's daughter Vady. Addison's grandchildren, as well as other family members, referred to Lucinda as Aunt Cindy.

Diane, Aunt Cindy Wilbanks Legg, Novel, June, and Butch

Lucy's Grandpa Legg and his second wife Aunt Cindy lived on the east side of Dan Walker's property. The old gray weathered house was made of vertical oak boards with another board nailed over the cracks. The small board and batten house was in the edge of the pasture across the road from where Dan and Vady Walker lived. Lucy said, "Grandpa Legg got cancer in his hand and first lost his fingers and then finally died." After a battle with cancer, Addison Laten Legg died on November 2, 1947.

Aunt Cindy continued to live in the old gray weathered house until her death. She had a big ugly brown dog called Brindly that took every step with her. After a visit with Grandma Vady, my sisters Diane and June and I had to walk Aunt Cindy home to make sure she got there ok. We would cross the dirt road then go by the south side of the milking barn and then cross the wide open pasture where we had to dodge all the big brown cow piles. The brown cow manure was usually dried and not near as bad as the green wet piles of crap. I remember stepping in the green cow piles while not paying attention to where I was putting my feet. Having that green stuff to squish up between my bare toes was not a good feeling.

According to my Aunt Lucille, "Aunt Cindy lived to about the1960's." Aunt Cindy's tombstone in the Friendship Baptist Church Cemetery on the west edge of Morgan County indicates she died on March 5, 1958. She was buried some three miles west of her home which was on Highway 41 at the Dan and Vady Walker place.

Katie Lucille identified the children of her parents Monroe Daniel (Dan) Walker and Maudy Nevady (Vady) Legg Walker, "My oldest Walker sibling was William Roy Walker. The other children were Thurman, Lora, Ida, Lodene, Paul, Brady, James, Violene, Oliver, Kenneth, and me, Katie Lucille. James and Lora passed away when they were young. My mother gave birth to fourteen children with two dying at childbirth, and two died young with one of them having scarlet fever and the other one was not a full term baby." The two young children Aunt Lucille was referring to were Lora who lived nearly one year and James who was premature and died after living only four days.

The young babies, Lora and James who passed away in early childhood, were buried at Friendship Baptist Cemetery at Upshaw in Winston County, and they have tombstones. It is thought that the two babies who were born dead were also buried at Friendship in unmarked graves. To distinguish the cemetery from others with the same name, family members referred to it as "Friendship on the Mountain." During the years that followed, many members of the Dan Walker family would be laid to rest at Friendship on the Mountain.

Chapter Two

Childhood Poverty

The difficulties of life during the 1930's placed extreme stress on parents as well as children. During the depression, most poor country families did not have the financial resources to afford proper medical care. It was not uncommon for women to give birth to their children at home without the assistance of a doctor. Many families during that time period had children who suffered diseases or die. Not only was proper medical care a concern, but adverse living conditions and poverty placed additional stress on the family.

The Dan Walker family was no exception. Maudy Nevady Walker gave birth to fourteen children at home. Although the Walker family suffered the loss of two babies that were still born and two that died as infants, ten of Dan and Vady's children eventually lived to adulthood. The two young babies that died after living for a short while were Lora and James. Lora Walker was less than a year old when she died of scarlet fever. Lora was born on August 12, 1915, and she died on August 1, 1916. After being born on March 1, 1927, James Walker was only four days old when he died on March 4, 1927. One of Katie Lucille's siblings, her brother Paul Walker, had polio that left him with a limp all his life.

At the time of Katie Lucille's birth, the Walker family was living in a one room log cabin located on the southeastern edge of Lawrence County, Alabama. When Vady gave birth to Lucy as with her other children, there was no medical doctor present. "We lived in that one room log cabin; my father did not own the house or land. There were nine kids at home living in that one room and that was not counting momma and daddy. Prior to William Roy Walker moving out, there were ten of us kids living together; Roy was my oldest brother and started working in a factory. After Roy got a job at the plant, he left the old log house and did factory work until he retired. Eventually, Thurmond built a house across the creek and he also left our home; we would cross the creek and go to Thurmond's home."

The Walker family did not have any modern conveniences while rearing their children. Katie Lucille said, "We had to wash our clothes in the creek on a rub board; we used lye soap to wash all the clothes." Lye soap was made with hog lard and water that had seeped through ashes from wood burning or from buying a can of Red Devil lye and mixing it with the hog lard. The ingredients were heated in a black cast iron pot and then allowed to cook forming the lye soap.

The family heated their home with wood or coal. Cooking was done on a black cast iron stove that had eyes that were covered with iron plates. There was no refrigerator, but later in Katie Lucille's childhood, the family had an ice box. In the summer time, items were kept cool by a large block of ice that was placed in the box. "We had no electricity, and I was twelve years old before we had electric power."

Although life during the depression was hard and getting by was just that, there were many wonderful things about living in the South especially in the spring and summer months. One advantage to growing up with a large family was having playmates.

Childhood years in the nineteen thirties were quite different. At that time, there were no televisions, I-pads, or video games. On those rare occasions when they were not working in the fields, the children played outside from daylight until dark. They ran barefoot in the yard, down the dirt road, and across newly plowed ground. Running barefoot was not a privilege, it was necessary because shoes were not always available. Yet, there was nothing to compare to frolicking barefoot across newly plowed fields and feeling the cool, soft, moist soil between their toes.

The siblings entertained themselves by batting rocks with sticks or kicking a tin can, if they could find a can, as they roamed down the dusty dirt roads. On rainy days, the children played in the rain, waded in the streams, and splashed in every mud puddle they could find. They stayed outside until dark catching lightening bugs, frogs, and crickets.

"The thing that blessed us little kids each week was the coke truck would come by our house. The driver would allow one or two bottles to fall out, and we would have ourselves an RC. We would wait for that truck to come by so we could get us a free cola. That was a thrill I had when I was a real small girl," Lucy said.

Even though she remembered pleasant events while growing up, she also had some terrifying memories. "I remember when I was real young we had a bad storm. I guess it was a tornado because it destroyed a lot of stuff." Since there was no electricity in her childhood days, the Walker family did not have television or radio to get tornado warnings. Katie Lucille also recalled other severe storms that occurred when she was a small child.

When Katie Lucille was a little girl, the family moved a few miles from the one room log cabin to another home. "We moved from the log cabin to Billy Goat Hill. I was three or four when we moved to Billy Goat Hill. It was a big old house. We had a hall, a bedroom, a fireplace, a kitchen, and the living room. In the one bedroom, we had mattresses and beds. When it got dark, we just went to bed."

Katie Lucille Walker's family moved from Billy Goat Hill to a farm her dad had purchased on an old Indian trail that locally ran from Jasper to Decatur. The aboriginal Indian path was one route of the Nashville-Mobile traces, and it became known as the Old Jasper Road. Later, the roadway became known as the Danville Road and eventually Highway 41. Lucy's family farm was on Highway 41 just one fourth mile south of the intersection of present-day Highway 157.

Lucy said, "Dad never owned land until he bought 139 acres on Danville Road which became Highway 41 in Morgan County about five miles south of Danville School. When he bought the land, everything was all grown up. Dad and all us kids cleared the land of trees."

In order to survive, Dan Walker was a hard working farmer. He expected hard work from all his children. Lucy said, "We cleaned up the land and planted corn and cotton. We all worked hard just to make sure we had enough to eat; we raised our own food."

The forested area was cleared of trees by Dan Walker and his children. They used the lumber from the oak trees that had been cut from the land to build a house on the west side of the road and a huge barn to the east of the road. After clearing the land on the farm he had purchased on Old Jasper Road, Dan selected the low flat ground on the east side of the road as his pasture land. The cropland was on a rolling hillside on the west side of the road that ran through the farm.

The crop land was terraced to prevent it from washing during heavy rain fall. The flat pasture land was fenced with barbed wire and was used as grazing for his cows and mules.

According Aunt Lucille, "The road that passed through our farm was just a rough wagon road on what became present-day Highway 41." In the early 1950's, it was just a dirt road full of mud holes in the early spring. The house and crop land was on the west side of the road and the milking barn and pasture was on the east side. The front yard of home was shaded by a big oak tree with massive limbs reaching across the dirt road. Dan kept his farming equipment stored under that big oak tree.

Katie Lucille's Parents

Katie Lucille's mom called her husband Mr. Dan; in turn, her dad called his wife Miss Vady. Those were the names that Mr. Dan and Miss Vady used when they were talking about each other or to each other. Their neighbors and fellow church members also called Lucy's parents Mr. Dan and Miss Vady.

Katie Lucille's parents were "born again Christians." They were Southern Baptist who practiced their religious beliefs. Dan, Vady, and the children went to the Baptist church on a regular basis. When Lucy was a little girl, the most vivid memory that she had of her father Dan Walker was that he was a preacher. Dan was noted for his preaching and church building in rural Morgan, Lawrence, and Winston Counties of North Alabama. "My father was a preacher. That is how I remember him when I was a young girl. The first church I remember going to was Friendship Baptist when I was about nine or ten years old. Daddy was preaching at that church," Lucy said.

Lucy's father did not receive pay for his preaching activities, but did get help from the people who attend the church services to hear his sermons. Aunt Lucille recalled, "They did not pay preachers then. Every once in a while they would have a pounding. One Sunday, they would say Mr. Dan and Miss Vady are running short so bring a pound of flour, a pound of sugar, a pound of coffee, or a pound of whatever the Lord lays on your heart. I remember one Sunday a lady had made a beautiful handmade quilt for us; it was gorgeous."

The house that Katie Lucille grew up in was a frame house without a bathroom. She said, "We never had indoor plumbing or an indoor toilet." The home that Lucy lived in until her teenage years did not have plumbing with running water inside their house; therefore, Mr. Dan and Miss Vady did not have a bathroom or commode while their children were living at home. Aunt Lucille said, "Prior to momma's death, I had an indoor bathroom installed in their house. Dad told me that Miss Vady could use the indoor outhouse, but he intended to keep using the outhouse on the outside."

Old habits are hard to break especially with a streak of Walker stubbornness attributed to Scots Irish ancestry. Even though all his children had married and moved away from home, Dan planned to continue using the outdoor toilet which was some fifty yards southwest of their house. His big outhouse accommodated three people at one time. In other words, it was a three holer that had been used for years by his large extended family. For several years following the installation of the indoor bathroom, Dan Walker continued to use the outhouse as his toilet. He also expected his visitors and family members to continue to use the outside outhouse.

Miss Vady

Mr. Dan and Miss Vady were strict parents, but Miss Vady gave her children much more freedom that Mr. Dan would allow, especially the girls. Lucy minded them, most of the time, without question. Lucy's mother was much more passive than her dad. Miss Vady's philosophy seemed to be, "Kids will be kids!" Miss Vady was not as demanding to her children as Mr. Dan, and she could be convinced to be more lenient especially with her youngest child Katie Lucille. Miss Vady was devoted to her sweet baby daughter, and in turn, Lucy adored her mother.

Miss Vady was a devout Christian who expected all those around her to be peace loving individuals, but she stood her ground when it came to right versus wrong. She always took a stand for what was right the way she saw it. She never raised her voice in anger, and she allowed her children more leeway in life than Mr. Dan as she always called him. She was dearly loved by her husband who had been known to give in to her demands although she rarely disputed his decisions. Miss Vady loved church, all day singings, and decorations with "Dinner on the

Ground" as church going southern people called it. She was a fun loving person who loved to laugh.

Miss Vady was a woman of great internal fortitude, but she had a much milder side than that of Mr. Dan. Miss Vady was rather short in statue, just under five feet tall, but not on strength as evidenced by the fourteen children she bore. She reared ten children to adulthood. She served as a strong role model for all of her children, grandchildren, and all that came in contact with her.

Miss Vady was well fitted for the role as a farmer's wife, and she was very active in farm life. She worked in the garden and kept food on the table. She took care of the hen house where

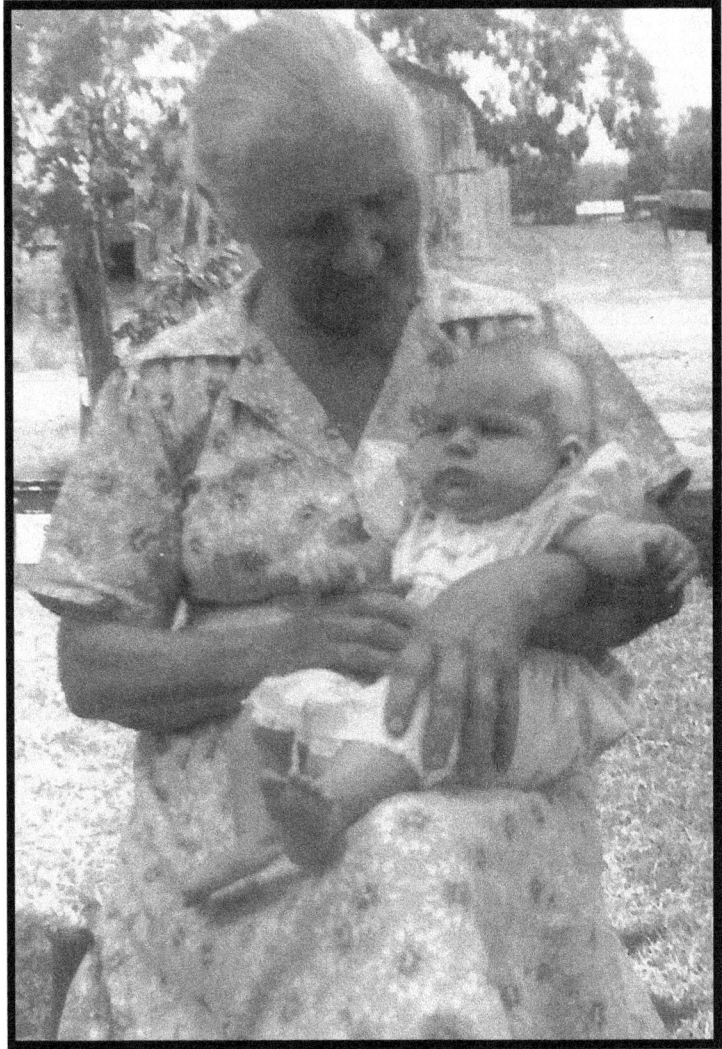

Ms. Vady held many babies and grandbabies

she daily gathered the eggs. Miss Vady had the primary use of the eggs for trading to the peddler for items she needed for the household. She could cook three meals each day on a wood burning stove, milk several head of cows at dawn and dusk, churn clabbered milk to make butter, grind peanuts into peanut butter, preserve and can all kinds of foods, sew all her family's clothes, make quilts for the beds, wash clothes in black iron pots, iron clothes with a flat iron that was heated on the stove top, and care for her home. Ms. Vady never complained, and her daughter Katie Lucille adopted that characteristic.

Miss Vady and all of her daughters never wore anything but a dress at the Dan Walker home. Katie Lucille said, "Dan Walker never allowed us girls to wear shorts or pants." In addition to her dresses, Miss Vady always wore a printed apron that was usually made from a flour sack. When she was working on the outside, she wore her bonnet. Miss Vady always wore her hair in a ball on the back of her head. It seemed that her hair had been white forever, but it was black in her younger years. Several of Miss Vady's children had black hair that would turn snow white in their old age.

Miss Vady was a woman who loved her Bruton snuff. She would hold two fingers making a "V-shape" against her lips and spit some fifteen feet. She would set on the front porch and never leave a drop of snuff juice on the floor; it all landed safely in the yard. She saved all her snuff jars and donated a set for drinking glasses to many of her children. If dipping snuff was a bad habit, it was the only one that Miss Vady had.

Miss Vady also had an artistic side. She loved making crepe paper flowers for the graves of her loved ones. Making crepe paper flowers was one of her many skills. Her ability as a seamstress was remarkable. She made all her children's clothing, and she taught her daughters and granddaughters to sew. Katie Lucille learned her mother's great ability to sew. Miss Vady, as well as her youngest daughter Lucy, was a self sufficient woman who stood by her man through thick and thin.

Mr. Dan

Dan Walker was a very strict man and only told his kids one time what he required. The second time meant serious consequences for the one who violated his rules. He was a tall muscular man with a dominating appearance. He was a Baptist preacher who did not tolerate foolishness or disobedience from his children or grandchildren.

Aunt Lucille told me, "Daddy never did yell at us; I do not remember him ever scolding me. I remember every day when he came in from farm work he would read to us from the Bible. Daddy made us a bench to go on one side of the table and chairs on the other side. Daddy would read the Bible and Brady would do his best to get me to laugh. Daddy would clear his throat, and I would have to swallow it."

Dan Walker had a Bible quote that he made sure that everyone in his family knew. The axiom of the Bible verse Proverbs 13:24 was *"Spare the rod and spoil the child."* However, according to my Aunt Lucille, Dan rarely used the rod, because he could usually control a situation by simply clearing his throat. But, I can attest to the fact that when Dan Walker decided it was time for the rod, he did such a good job that one would not want to take a chance of getting a second whipping.

Aunt Lucille Walker said, "I know of only two whippings daddy gave; one was to Oliver and the other was Brady. Brady got whipped with a brush broom. Brady and I were always into something. I remember when I was about fourteen, I got up that morning and Brady was on the porch sick. I went to daddy crying telling him Brady was sick. He told me to go on about my business and let Brady tend to his own self. I did not know until about a year after I was married that Brady had been out all night and was drunk. I did not know anything about beer, whiskey, or nothing like that. I asked mama after I was married what was wrong with Brady that time, and she whispered, 'He was drunk on beer, honey.'"

Sandy Welborn, Butch Walker, Danny Welborn

After Aunt Lucille was serving this great country in foreign lands as a soldier's

27

wife, my Grandpa Dan did some whippings that she had no knowledge of, but I can give a firsthand account. Danny Welborn, Sandy Welborn, and I were mischievous grandsons of Dan Walker. Danny and Sandy were double cousins and the sons of Willard Welborn and Lucy's sister Violene Walker Welborn.

Grandpa Dan had warned us about moving his farming equipment when we were playing under the big water oak tree in the front yard. After a few minutes, we forgot about the warning. We looked up and saw grandpa coming across the yard with his leather razor straps in hand. For those not familiar with the razor straps, they were three or more thick leather bands about three to four inches wide that were bound together at one end which usually had a wooden handle. The straps were used to sharpen a straight razor for shaving; however, it was grandpa's choice disciplinary tool. Seeing the razor straps, we all knew what was going to happen because he only gave one warning.

I looked at Danny and Sandy, and I could see the fear in their eyes. I was well aware of what was about to happen. Grandpa grabbed me under the arm and lifted me off the ground to the point that my toes were barley touching the dirt. With that leather razor strap, grandpa gave me one of the most memorable whippings that I got during my entire life. After Danny, Sandy, and I got that whipping, we were rubbing our burning butts for a long time. That leather strap always hung on the wall and was always a vivid reminder to take grandpa's warnings as serious as a coiled rattlesnake. Dan Walker was a stern man who demanded respect; he loved his family and their welfare was always his main concern. Still, he expected obedience.

Although Dan Walker disciplined his grandchildren, he also took time to play his favorite game with them. He was a master playing checkers. He had every move on the checker board all ready figured out before his opponent ever made a move. I played checkers with him many times, but I never beat him in a single game. He would smile real big when he would jump several of my checkers at one time. Needless to say, he always won.

My sister Diane Walker Thrasher would challenge Grandpa Dan in his checker game every once in a while. When she got him cornered, he would take a very long time calculating his next move. My sister said that she would get so tired sitting there at the checker board that she would count the nails in the ceiling of the room. The ceiling of the house was covered with sheetrock, but none of the nails heads had been plastered over and were visible. Grandpa Dan would clear his throat, place his hand on a checker, and contemplate his next move while Diane stared at the ceiling. Finally, he would make his calculated move.

According to Katie Lucille and related to her by her mother Vady, Dan Walker in his early years engaged in moon shining activities. At one point in his moon shining career, he used his gun to escape prosecution without killing the revenuers. From that time on, he never participated in the making of whiskey. He made a complete turnaround in life, and he began a career as a hell fire and brimstone Baptist preacher. Dan Walker helped establish churches in the surrounding area. Although he was a preacher, Dan Walker had a confrontation to the point that someone's life was threatened.

According to a story told by my dad Brady Walker, the old twelve gauge shotgun that Dan Walker owed was used to back up his statements. Most of the following incident was told to me by my dad who was the brother of Katie Lucille Walker. Bits and pieces of the story came from my Walker uncles who had to endure all my questions to satisfy the curiosity of their young nephew who wanted to know about his family history and heritage.

One of Dan Walker's teenage daughters became involved with a man that he thought was a bad influence. Dan felt that the man was taking advantage of his daughter. He was intent on putting a stop to the problems the young man was causing for the Walker family. It appeared to Dan that the young man had convinced his daughter to shack up without being married. Of course, a hell fire and brimstone old timey Baptist preacher could not let the family be disgraced and disrespected by such a scandal.

Dan Walker, armed with his shotgun, got his oldest son William Roy Walker, who was also armed with a shotgun, to go with him to confront the young man who was making a mockery of the family. When they approached the house, Dan told his daughter to come outside and wait until he took care of business with her suitor. Dan told his daughter that he would talk to her when they got home. Dan and his oldest son William Roy Walker entered the house. Dan Walker had a very serious *"Come to Jesus"* talk with the young fellow who was misleading his daughter.

**Standing L-R: Dan, Roy, Oliver, Lodean, Thurman, Ida, Vady
Squatting: Brady, and Paul - missing are Violene, Kenneth, Lucille**

Brady Walker said, "I thought that dad had actually killed the man and hid his body." For many years, no one heard from the guy that was shacked up with his sister. After graduating from college and getting a job, I went by one day to visit with my dad Brady. He commenced to tell me what had happen that day. He started off by saying, "Do you have any idea who I saw today?"

My dad was always asking questions and seemed to expect me to know the answers even though I had no idea what he was talking about. I told Brady, "How do you expect me to know who you saw today because I have no idea where you have been?"

At that point, Brady Walker began to relate the entire story about one of his sisters. He called the man by name and told that he always thought the man had been killed. Brady said, "I was at the store today when I got to talking to this gentleman that I thought I did not know. After we talked a while, I found out he was the man that I thought dad had killed." I could tell that Brady was extremely surprised that the man was still alive. Brady told that shortly after the altercation that Dan Walker had with the young suitor, that the young man moved up north where he had lived most of his life.

Brady Walker jokingly told the man, "You better be glad you left this part of the country."

He said the gentleman replied, "I know Mr. Dan Walker meant what he said, and I was not about to take any chances!"

Dan Walker was a man of powerful words. He lived most of his life as a servant of God, but people took his stern demeanor as a statement of strength. One could look at his eyes and see the fear of God. To say that Dan Walker was intimidating in expression and appearance was an understatement.

Dan Walker lived by his strict religious interpretation of the *Holy Bible*. He insisted that his children and grandchildren live up to his expectations regarding their behavior and appearance if they were in his presence or at his house. Dan's standards were also applied to how his children dressed and what they wore.

"Even when we helped in the fields with plowing or picking cotton, we were required to wear dresses. Even after I got married, I was not allowed at Dan Walker's house in shorts. I guess growing up in that culture is the reason I feel uncomfortable wearing shorts today. In addition, daddy would never let one of his girls wear pants because it said in the Bible for women not to wear men's clothes. If we wore stockings, it was mamas brown stockings. We worked in the fields in dresses. We milked cows in a dress. We did everything in a dress," Katie Lucille remarked.

Dan Walker would not allow Aunt Lucille to wear shorts at his house even though she was an adult woman. She said, "I was married and had three children when I and Asa came home from Germany to visit the family. One morning while we were home with mother and dad, I was outside washing clothes in shorts when dad saw me. He told me that he did not allow women at his house to go naked. He pointed out that the school bus would be passing his house in a few minutes and he expected me to be dressed. I quickly, honored dad's wishes, and I went in the house and put on a skirt over my shorts even though the shorts were down to my knees."

Ida, Lodean, Vady, Lucy, and Violine Walker

Dan was so strict that he refused to allow his daughters to wear pants. He seemed to be of the opinion that wearing shorts or pants would surely send his girls to hell, and he wanted them to join him in the promise land.

Dan Walker had very strong old timey Baptist beliefs and preached his strict philosophy to saint and sinner alike. He believed that sparing the rod would spoil the child. Lucy and all his other children were well informed and knew first hand of the consequences for violating the rules he viewed as scriptural.

After retiring from full time ministry, Dan would preach his beliefs from his front porch every Sunday afternoon. He expected his children and grandchildren to attend Sunday dinner and listen to his sermons after eating. The Walker children would gather on a regular basis at the Dan Walker home on Sunday afternoons for the traditional family dinner.

After a great meal, Dan would begin his front porch Sunday afternoon sermons which would last for hours. Very few ever questioned his authority on the word of God, and if they did, they could feel the hell fire and brimstone coming from his Bible lesson delivered on his front porch.

Anyone who had ever heard Dan Walker talking about hell would not want to go there. If someone wore something or did something he did not like, Dan would preach a sermon about the sins that would send one straight to hell. When he preached about the many lost souls and their wicked ways, Dan Walker could make a person feel like he was knocking on the gates of Hades and shaking hands with the devil.

Never did anyone challenge Dan Walker's teachings because he was going to lose the argument. While growing up, Dan Walker's children and grandchildren had to listen for hours to his sermons because someone would ask a question about the Bible. Whether one wanted to hear about hell fire and brimstones, he knew better than leaving during Dan's front porch preaching because that would have been disrespectful. Dan did not allow disrespecting elders at his house. Everyone knew better than to cross that line. Dan Walker believed in *Proverbs 22: 6*, "Train up a child in the way he should go, and he will not depart from it."

Farm Life

During the 1930's, growing-up on a farm in the rural south usually meant living in close proximity to a small country town. The closest town to the Walker farm was Hartselle, Alabama, which was located at the junction of the present Highways 31 and 36. Katie Lucille remembered Highway 36 as a dusty rough road that ran from Wren in Lawrence County to Morgan County passing through Danville and Hartselle. Portions of the road were originally an old Indian trail that was known as the Coosa Path or the Muscle Shoals Path. In early settler days, the road east and west through Hartselle was also known historically as the Moulton to Somerville Road via Irwin's Mill.

Katie Lucille said, "I remember when I was five years old that dad was doing business with Bennett and Stewart in Hartselle. They had the bank; they had everything we needed on the farm to survive." Farming and planting activities required the Walker family to purchase supplies at Hartselle. Supplies such as plow boots, tools, fertilizer or guano, and other things for planting the corn, cotton, as well as other items needed on the farm were purchased in Hartselle.

33

The Walker family did not spend a lot of money buying food and clothes at the store or in town. They raised most of their food and made their own clothes. Aunt Lucille said, "White flour sacks were our sheets. Unless daddy had guano sacks to make clothes; flour sacks were our panties and slips; that is what I wore to school. We had princess style dresses, gored at the bottom just below the knee. That is all we had."

In addition to manure, commercial fertilizer or guano was bought in Hartselle and used when planting cotton and corn. The cloth sacks that contained the fertilizer were used to make sheets, pillow cases, underwear, and clothes. All the babies at that time had diapers made from sacks that had contained fertilizer or flour. I was no exception. When I was a baby, mother and Grandma Vady used the sacks to make my diapers.

Katie Lucille said, "When I was a child, we did not have a washer. We had that big well. We had to draw water to put in the pots. A fire was built around two of the pots; we washed our clothes on a scrub board in one and rinse in the other two. We would hang the wet clothes out on a line to dry. I didn't complain; I would just do it."

By the late 1950's, the family no longer had to wash their clothes in the creek on a rub board. Although the family had an electric wringer washing machine on the back porch, Vady was still washing some of the clothes on the outside. For overalls and other heavy clothes with deep stains, she used scrub or rub boards and those three big cast iron black pots. Water was drawn from the big hand dug well in a bucket to fill the pots. Two pots had fires built around their bases so the clothes could be washed in hot water. One pot was filled with cold water for the final rinsing.

One of the heated pots was used with the scrub board and lye soap for washing their clothes. Lye soap, which was made from hog fat, was used to clean the clothes. The scrub board had parallel ridges; it was placed into one of the pots and the clothes were rubbed up and down across the ridges until they were clean. The other heated pot was used for the first rinse with the cold water pot for the final rinse. Once the clothes were washed, they were hung outside on the clothes line to air dry.

In addition to being a Baptist preacher, Dan Walker was a farmer all his life. Several acres of crop land were planted every spring. The main cash crop was cotton. Corn was used to feed the hogs, chickens, cows, mules, and ground into meal for cornbread. Peanuts were eaten fresh, roasted, or turned into peanut butter. Sugar cane was used to make molasses. Fruits of all kinds were dried on the roof of sheds. A garden provided all kinds of vegetables that were either eaten fresh or canned in mason jars.

Dan Walker had mules, a bunch of milk cows, hogs, chickens, redbone hound dogs, and fruit trees. Everything on the farm had a purpose and was utilized by the family to survive. Mules were used to plow the fields. Hogs were killed every year for meat. Chickens provide meat and eggs. Redbone hound dogs were used to catch coons and possums.

Fruit trees produced peaches, apples, cherries, figs, and plums that could be eaten fresh or dried on top of the chicken pen roof. After the fruit was dried, it was placed in a pillow case or cloth bag and hung in a dry place until it was used in pies. Lucy recalled, "We would pick apples and peaches from the fruit trees to making jellies and jams in addition to drying the fruit; we made molasses." The molasses were made from sugar cane grown on the Walker farm.

Cows were milked and the milk was used to drink fresh, make butter, or sold. Aunt Lucille said, "Mamma and us kids would churn clabbered milk to make our butter; she would grind the peanuts we raised to make peanut butter."

Each year before farming and planting time, the manure was dug out of the barn stalls and shoveled on to the wagon. When the wagon was full of cow manure, it was taken to the crop land and spread over the fields. Dan Walker's old barn was gray from years of weathering. The barn was made by him and his children and covered with tin. The floors of the barn were dirt, but would fill up with cow patties, mule manure, and hay. Every year the manure would build up in the barn. The manure had to be shoveled out and hauled away to the cotton and corn patches.

A lot of cow and mule manure was used to fertilize the garden. A big garden was planted every spring; it provided food that allowed the Walker family survived without making frequent trips to the store. Onions, cabbage, radishes, beets, sweet corn, potatoes, tomatoes, okra, squash, collards, cantaloupes, watermelons, and various kinds of other vegetables were planted in the garden. Most of the vegetables were eaten fresh or canned.

Canning required the vegetables to be placed in mason jars with lids, then heated in a cold pack or pressure cooker on the wood burning stove. After the jars cooled which caused them to seal, they were stored for the winter time dinner table.

In addition to preserving vegetables, the Walkers would process their own meat. Since the family butchered their own pork, black cast iron pots were very important while processing hogs. Katie Lucille said, "We killed hogs!" The coming of fall put everyone on lookout for the first killing frost. A cold frosty morning meant that it was time to kill the fattened hogs for the winter's meat supply. Although cold mornings made everyone want to stay in bed, farm families knew this was time for hog killing work. On the cold morning, preparations began early.

First fires had to be built under large pots so boiling water would be ready. Lucy's family used the three big, black cast iron wash pots that fires were built around in order to have hot water for hog killing time. Hot water from one of the pots was used to scald the hog so that the hair could be easily scraped off with big butcher knives.

Another pot was used to heat the hog skin and fat to turn it into cracklings and lard. The lard was used for cooking and soap making. Much of the lard was put in metal cans and used during the year for cooking the family meals. The rest of the heated lard was mixed with lye in one of the pots to make lye soap. Once cooled, the solid lye soap was taken out and cut into blocks to be used for washing clothes and bathing.

Some of the hog meat was used fresh for eating. Much of the meat was hand ground and made into sausage. The hide and skin was used for making cracklings and pork skins which were delicious when eaten fresh. The hams were hung in the smoke house and smoked with hickory or pecan wood.

The sides of the hog were called middlings. They were cut into bacon or placed in the salt box and covered with salt to be preserved. Before the sides of bacon were eaten in the spring, sometimes little worms called zippers would bore holes through the meat. The family still ate it even though it was very strong with a slight rancid taste. Dan Walker said those holes in the bacon are not going to hurt anybody.

The hog head and other parts were turned into souse mean. The Walker table usually had souse meat with pepper sauce and crackers. All the hog's internal organs including the heart, liver, lungs, kidneys, and intestines were eaten. Boiled hog lungs were called lights and were eaten by the Walker family.

Aunt Lucille helped with all the hog killing activities including making chitlings from the intestines. The hot chitlings were good when just taken out of the pot of boiling grease; but, once they got cold, the smell and thought of eating hog guts was not real appetizing. Some of the Walker family also liked the mountain oysters that are cooked boar hog testicles.

In addition to helping with hog killing, gathering eggs was among Katie Lucille's other chores. "We had a chicken house and chickens of all kinds; daddy built a hen house for them with nests." Dan and his boys had built a big chicken pen with roosts and nest boxes. Lucy enjoyed going to the hen house to pick up eggs, but she had to be very careful not to break any of those valuable eggs that her mother would trade to the peddler. Meeting the peddler was a big thrill for the Walker children; sometimes they even got candy or ice cream. The peddler would come by in his big ole panel truck filled with everything one could find in a modern day Wal-Mart; that may be stretching the truth, but the peddler had about everything country folks needed to survive.

"We would trade eggs for anything that the peddler had. We had a lot of laying chickens, so mama could get a lot of stuff she needed by trading eggs. Every Saturday after we got a vehicle, daddy would go to Lonnie Morris's store and get all of us an RC Cola. Everything else that we needed, we got from the peddler. The peddler carried cloth or material to make dresses and clothes or anything else we needed. Mama would get material and needles and thread from the peddler. She would make all her own dress patterns and made us beautiful dresses," Katie Lucille remembered.

"My family survived the depression through hard work and self sufficiency. I lived that way because that is the only way I knew," Lucy stated!

Cotton Farming

Katie Lucille's father farmed for a living. "We farmed with mules for a long time; we had a pair of gray mules. Then daddy bought a tractor. Everybody worked, but if we would have work the next day, Oliver would say, 'I am gonna have a headache tomorrow,' and Violene would say, 'Oh my back is gonna be killing me tomorrow.' Those two siblings of mine did not like the hard farm work."

The cotton field had to be kept clear of grass and weeds. Since herbicides did not exist when Katie Lucille and her siblings were young, they had to use a hoe to clear the rows of cotton of trash plants that would stunt the cotton stalks and reduce production. Chopping or hoeing cotton was one of the toughest jobs on the farm. Not only did the field have to be cleared of undesirable plants, the cotton had to be thinned so it could grow bigger and produce more cotton. Hoeing usually started at daylight and ended at dark. The cotton fields had to be hoed two to three times during the season.

Hoeing in the fields whether it was hoeing corn or chopping cotton was tiring work especially on long, hot, humid days. One day while hoeing cotton, Katie Lucille's brother Brady remembered an old tale claiming that if someone caught a cricket and buried it alive there would be a rain. Some people, including the Walker children, believed that old tale to be true. On one of those very hot, dry, sultry days of summer, Brady decided to put the old tale on trial. He began talking to his brother Kenneth about catching a cricket. Brady reminded Kenneth of the story about burying a cricket alive to bring rain so they could get some relief from their tiring job of chopping cotton.

Since their dad was hoeing right along with them, Brady and Kenneth began working a little slower and lagging behind. Their dad suspected that something was in the making so he cleared his throat as he always did before sounding a warning for the boys to keep up. Then sure enough, Kenneth found a cricket and handed it to Brady who dug a hole and buried the cricket alive. In a little while, the sun went behind the clouds, and a breeze swept across the cotton patch. The boys giggled, and their dad cleared his throat loudly warning them to keep up and pay attention to the cotton they were hoeing. The wind picked up. The clouds gathered. The sky darkened, and a few drops of rain began to fall.

Worrying about the cricket tale, Kenneth told Brady to ask dad if they could go to the house. Dad's answer was, "Keep hoeing boys, there's more work to be done." The sky grew darker, the wind blew harder, thunder could be heard in the distance, and more drops of rain fell. Worrying about the buried cricket, again Brady asked if they could go to the house. Being a man of few words, dad's answer was, "Keep hoeing boys." Suddenly a huge gust of wind swept across the cotton field, and a streak of lightening flashed across the black sky. Thunder roared; lightening flashed; rain poured from the dark clouds. Dad said, "Now you boys can go to the house." The boys stood their hoes in the dirt to mark their spot and began running toward the house. Looking back, they saw the lightening strike Brady's hoe handle and bust it into splinters. Needless to say, Lucy's brothers never buried another cricket alive.

In addition to hoeing the cotton, the Walker children had to help with cultivation of the crops. Katie Lucille told about using mules to farm the cotton crop. Mules were used to work the land and for maintenance of the row crops. Georgia stock middle busters, sweeps, and scratchers were metal plows that were pulled by the mules to clear the weeds and grass from the middle between the rows of cotton, corn, or other crops. Dan Walker and his boys were usually doing the cultivating of

Brady Walker

the fields with the mules. One could hear the gees and haws ringing from the boys loudly hollering at the old mules in order for them to go left or right.

While cultivating the cotton crops, Brady would use some choice words on those mules that were unacceptable to Dan Walker, but he knew better than to use those cuss words in the presence of his dad. One day the mule was acting up and being unruly. While his brother held the scratcher and continued to cultivate the cotton, Brady went to the house for something. With no idea what Brady was up to, it did not take long to find out. While trying to keep the stubborn old mule in the middle of the row to prevent him from destroying the cotton plants, all of a sudden to the mule's complete surprise, Brady hit that mule upside the head with a board. Of course, the mule took off running across the field with the Georgia stock just bouncing along behind. One can only imagine the damage done to the cotton crop by a runaway mule attached to a plow.

When working on the farm, it was customary for the Walker boys to wear overalls. Aunt Lucille said, "Brady and all my brothers wore overalls when they were growing up. The boys had knee pads they wore to pick cotton, but I just bent over while picking. I was about five when I started picking cotton. The sack I used when I picked cotton was eight feet long. I was a good cotton picker. I do not know why, but God just made me where I could just pick cotton."

During the time Katie Lucille was picking cotton on her parents' farm, mechanical cotton picking machines did not even exist. Picking cotton by hand was not the easiest job on the farm. Each boll of cotton had burrs that would make the fingers sore and bleed. The person picking cotton would have to bend over at the waist or crawl on their knees to get the cotton in reach of their fingers; knees and backs would get sore at the end of a twelve hour day.

Each picker would have a six to nine foot long sack that could hold some one hundred pounds. The sack had a strap that went over the shoulder and would aid in pulling the sack up and down the cotton rows. As the cotton sack became filled with cotton, it was harder to pull and cause the shoulder to hurt because of the extra weight. Once the sack was full, it was picked up and placed on top of the shoulder to be carried to the wagon where it was weighed.

Katie Lucille said, "Brady and I could pick three hundred eighty to four hundred pounds of cotton a day; we could pick cotton very fast. Brady and I would run off down the cotton rows and leave Kenneth and Violene; we would leave our other brothers and sisters behind."

The farmers kept a log book with the name of everyone who was picking cotton in order to record the poundage of cotton in each sack that was weighed. When Aunt Lucille was picking cotton on the family farm in the 1940's, she or her siblings did not get paid. If the Walker children hired out to pick cotton for another farmer, they were paid from seventy five cents to one dollar per hundred pounds of cotton picked.

Most of the time during the 1950's, farmers paid from one dollar and seventy five cents to two dollars and fifty cents per hundred pounds of cotton picked. A young quick cotton picker during the 1950's was lucky to make five dollars per day for picking cotton. At the end of the day, everyone would line up to be paid based on the number of pounds of cotton picked. The cotton farmers usually paid their field hands in cash for their day of work.

After the cotton was weighed, it was emptied into the bed of the wagon that had sideboards some four feet high. Most wagons would hold about one bale of cotton. Once the cotton was ginned free of seeds and trash, the clean bale would usually weigh about five hundred or more pounds.

The day of cotton picking usually started at daylight and ended near dark. During the 1940's and 1950's, school was dismissed for six weeks during the fall for cotton picking season so children could help harvest the cotton before winter set in. Many days, it would be freezing cold in the early morning hours, but before the day was over, everyone was wet with sweat.

Aunt Lucille said, "I was the best picker we had. Some days, I would pick four hundred pounds of cotton. I was a teenager when I first started picking four hundred pounds of cotton each day. That Brady would say, 'Ok sis if you beat me picking cotton today, I will pay you a quarter.'"

The cotton picking day usually started after breakfast at the first rays of daylight. They would quit picking just before dark after being in the cotton patch for about twelve hours. The family would take a short break each day at noon to eat dinner. They only took just enough time to finish their meal then they all headed back to the cotton patch.

"While we were at lunch after picking cotton all morning, Brady would say, 'Now sis, I need you to shine my shoes because I am going out tonight' or 'Sis, I will give you a quarter to draw my bath water.' We had a lot of big tubs that we would fill with water so that the water could get warm in the sun. Then in the evening, we would have warm water to take a bath. I never did get any quarters. He never paid me, and he would say, 'I will pay you next time.' I believed him. We just had a great time."

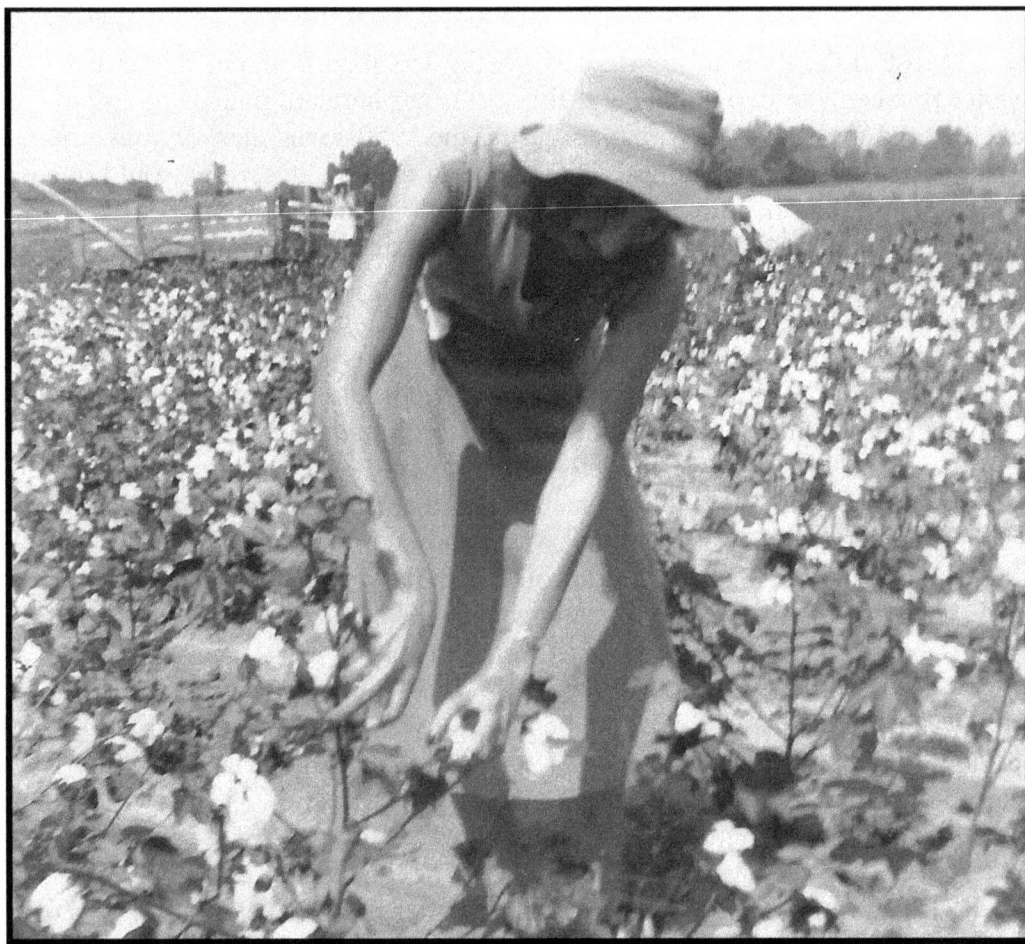

Lucy Walker picking cotton

When Aunt Lucille was picking cotton, the Walker family did not have farm trucks or tractors. Everything on the farm was accomplished using mules for all farming activities. Two mules were used to pull the cotton wagon. As cotton was placed in the wagon, the farmer or his paid hands would get in the wagon and stomp the cotton until it was packed as tight as they could get it. Children loved to help pack the cotton and jump off the highest part of the wagon into the soft, fluffy cotton.

The wagon had to have at least one bale of cotton before it was taken to the cotton gin. A trip to the gin with mules pulling the wagon was an all day affair. Sometimes ginning would require an overnight stay if a lot of wagons were in line at the gin.

Most children loved riding and sleeping in the cotton wagon waiting for the gin workers to get to their wagon. They also enjoyed watching the men operating the big suction tube to get the cotton out of the wagon. After a long wait during the ginning process, children would usually get a coke for a nickel and wait for their dad to get his check and the seed. The cotton seed was not only used for planting the next year, but was also a great feed for Dan Walker's milk cows.

Lucy said, "My first trip to town was to the cotton gin in Hartselle with daddy. I was about nine years old. I remember two times when dad would let me ride in the cotton wagon with him to Hartselle to the gin. The wagon held a bale of cotton and us. It was a long skinny wagon that had two sets of wheels with spokes, and it was pulled by two horses. I sat on a seat in the front. It took us all day to make the trip from Danville to Hartselle."

Hartselle was just a small country town that had grown up at a road junction and a railroad. In the early 1940's, the thriving little town had a train depot, a doctor's office, a post office, a bank, a couple of dry goods stores and, of course, a hardware store. Stewart and Bennett Hardware store carried everything from water buckets and dippers to cotton seed and hoes.

Dan Walker conducted his business in Hartselle. Needless to say as a young girl, Katie Lucille was excited when she was given permission to go to the cotton gin in Hartselle with her dad. Years later in that small Morgan County town, she would meet the man who would become her husband, and she would become a soldier's wife.

Milking Cows

Although, he supervised all his farming operations, Dan Walker was not one to milk the cows. Yet, he had some forty milk cows which were milked by hand. He never owned milking machines; there was nothing modern about the milking activities. He thought milking was a job for women and children; therefore, Vady and the children had to do all the milking.

The cows were placed in individual stalls, and they were given some feed that was put in a wooden trough. While the cows ate their food, Lucy and her siblings would milk them by pulling on their teats.

Aunt Lucille said, "When I was about thirteen years old, I started milking the cows. Every morning before we went to school, we had to hand milk the forty head of cows. We carried a bucket of clean water to wash the cow's teats, a stool to set on, and a bucket to hold the fresh milk."

Everybody except Dan was expected to do their share of milking and the pay they got for the job was food on the table and fresh milk to drink. Sometimes the milk was bitter or strong tasting because the cows would eat bitter weeds or wild onions, but the family members drank it anyway.

Some of the milk was used to make butter. The milk was allowed to clabber, and then it was placed in the churn. Most of the children got the opportunity to work the dasher up and down in the churn until the butter formed on top of the liquid. Vady would scoop off the butter and place in a mold to solidify and what was left was used as butter milk. A big bowl of butter milk and hot cornbread made a great meal. It was even better when a garden fresh onion or tomato was added to the bowl of cornbread and buttermilk.

Vady Walker and her children, including Katie Lucille and my dad Brady, helped with the milking activities. As a little boy, I remember watching my Grandma Vady milking the old cows. As she sat on the three legged wooden stool, I would ask for a drink of warm milk. Grandma would tell me to open my mouth wide. She would then direct one of the cow's teats in my direction and squirt milk in my mouth. She rarely missed my mouth. It was also in that old milking barn that Brady taught me how to milk the cows.

Most of the fresh milk from the Dan Walker dairy operation was sold to the Carnation Milk Company. Katie Lucille said, "I did whatever my brothers and sisters did, and in later years when some married and mother got bursitis, me and Kenneth would get up about four in the morning and milk about twenty five to thirty head of cows. We sold milk to the Carnation Company. We milked the cows in the morning, picked cotton during the day, and milked the cows again that evening."

The milk had to be prepared and poured into large metal cans for the morning pickup by the milk company. Lucy recalled, "After we milked a cow, we would pour the bucket of milk through a big wire strainer lined with a clean flour sack into the milk can. Then we would milk another cow and follow the same procedure. We had to strain all the fresh milk prior to putting it into the metal milk cans. After school, we were again at the barn milking the old cows before supper, but the milk in the afternoon was placed in gallon jugs. The jugs of milk were place in lard buckets that were set in the pond to keep cool."

Since the Walker family did not own a cooler, placing the containers of milk in the pond was the only way to keep it cool. If the milk set in the heat all night, it would turn sour or blink. According to Lucy, "During the next morning, the afternoon milk would be placed in the big metal milk cans along with the fresh milk. Every morning we milked all those old cows that dad had in his small dairy operation. We put the milk into big metal cans and placed the milk cans on the side of the road to be sold. The milk truck would come by on a regular basis to pick up the milk and then send dad a check."

Chapter Three

Katie's School Days

The good Lord granted Katie Lucille (Lucy) Walker an enormous amount of ambition which she did not hide under a bush. Her work ethic was greater than the majority of school girls or boys her age. In all the chores or work that was assigned, she did much more than was required or asked. She, like most of her brothers and sisters, attended Danville School.

As the youngest of fourteen children, Lucy had a desire to prove she was worthy. She wanted to show her older siblings and friends that she could do more than they could. It may have been that she knew that she was the baby. Lucy seemed to have a need for recognition that she was as capable as the first born child in the family or as intelligent as any of her school friends.

Katie Lucille Walker thought that some of her siblings were jealous of her as the baby child. She said, "One of the first things I remember was my siblings thinking I was a spoiled brat. The most important thing about me was if I saw something that needed to be done, I just did it. They thought I was trying to be smart, but I was not."

Katie Lucille Walker was a very competitive person, and she had the desire to succeed. Pleasing her dad and mom was the motivation for her hard work ethic as a young girl, and she wanted to do things better than her siblings and friends. She was intent on having the admiration of others through her outgoing personality and strong work ethic. All through her life, Katie Lucille demonstrated her will and determination to be successful in what she did.

Katie Lucille knew that she did not have fine clothes, shoes, and money that others would admire. She also knew that she was just a poor farm girl who had big dreams that she was determined to fulfill. Therefore, to get the favorable recognition of friends and family, she had the will to achieve more and out work her peers and siblings. She not only wanted to be successful in all tasks, but Lucy had the desire to be the best in all that she attempted. She was as highly motivated in school as she was in picking cotton.

46

The times were extremely hard when Lucy was attending the first years of school. She had to face many challenges of poverty related to the Great Depression prior to completing elementary school. She was the youngest child with nine older siblings who lived through the great economic collapse of our country. During the worst time of the Great Depression, the Walker family often had nothing to eat for breakfast but cornbread and molasses.

Many times, the only thing that Katie Lucille and her siblings had to eat for lunch at Danville School was one of her mother's big biscuits which she took in a tin pail. Like other women of her generation, Vady Walker cooked with lard and made big, fat, fluffy biscuits that would completely fill a person's stomach. Lucy was just happy to have that big biscuit in her syrup bucket, and she was not embarrassed by her family's poor economic circumstances.

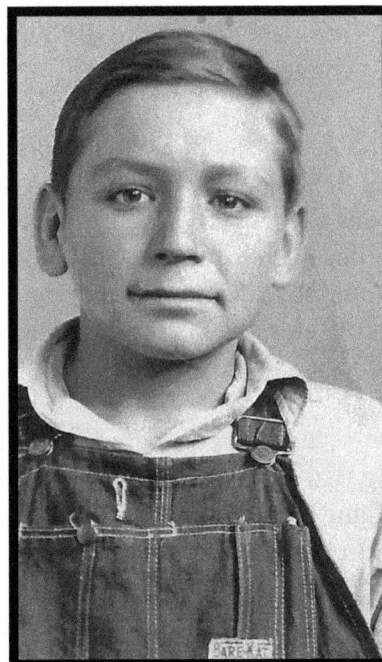

SCHOOL DAYS
1939 - 40

Brady Walker

Most of the Walker children went to school at Danville which was located some five miles north of their home at the junction of Highway 41 and Highway 36. The Walker boys wore used and passed down brogans (plow boots) and overalls to school during those severe economic times. Lucy's brother Brady Walker is pictured at Danville High School wearing overalls and a homemade shirt when he was fourteen years old.

Katie Lucille and her older sisters wore dresses that were homemade by their mother. She knew that the family could not afford the fine clothes that some of the other children wore, but she did not complain. Lucy was proud to wear the homemade clothes that her mother had sewed.

The Walker girls and boys wore plow boots to school that were passed down when they got too small for the older children. It was customary for the

47

older children pass down their work boots to their younger siblings. Each of the Walker children had only one pair of shoes to wear. They had to wear the same pair of shoes to school that they wore to the cotton fields.

Katie Lucille said, "I first went to school at Danville. I wore my dresses and Kenneth's boots. Sometimes I did not even have socks to wear, but it did not bother me." Lucy was just happy to have the opportunity to go to school. She had a strong outgoing personality and a tremendous amount of self confidence; therefore, what she wore did not impact her in a negative way and was not her main concern.

Lucy said, "I would wear the boys plow boots when I attended Danville High School. I had one pair of shoes and was blessed. Most of the time, I wore Kenneth's brogans; I did not have Sunday shoes." Like many other small farm families during the depression, the Walker family had virtually no money. The little money they had was spent on necessities, and Sunday shoes were certainly not considered a necessity. Life was tough and everybody in the country did what was necessary to survive.

"I made good grades; I only remember getting in trouble one time. One thing that stands out in my mind is I memorized all the beatitudes of the Bible in first and second grades. I still know them. I just have to get my mind on it, but when I glance over them I know them," recalled Lucy.

Not only did the Walker children have the Bible read to them at home by their father, they also studied the Bible at school. It is sad today that children are not taught about the Bible at school because our country of the United States was founded on Biblical principles.

"Miss Lucille Livingston was my teacher in first grade; she was a good teacher. My second grade teacher was Ms. Wiggins, and she is still alive. My third grade teacher was Ms. Lindsay. She was an old maid and never married. She lived in a little house outside of Danville. In the fifth grade, the school burned, and we went to school at the Methodist church in Danville. All my high school years were at Danville," recalled Katie Lucille. The school was rebuilt after the fire, and Lucy and her siblings continued their education at Danville School.

Many kids would walk several miles to school during pretty warm weather, but some farmers like Dan Walker would convert their farm trucks to school buses during the winter months. Dan Walker purchased a flat bed Dodge farm truck, and he would use it as a school bus for his children and some of the neighboring children to ride to school. Katie Lucille and other children that lived in the area would ride that truck to school. Dan was not compensated for the use of his truck or his time, but his children did not have to walk to school during bad weather.

In the 1940's, there were few opportunities for girls to participate in sports, but Danville School did have a girls' basketball team. Lucy loved to play basketball, and she was good enough to make the girls' basketball team. Girl basketball players at Danville High School were required to wear shorts.

Since playing basketball meant wearing shorts, Lucy knew that her daddy would not let her play. She knew that her daddy did not allow his daughters to wear shorts, so Lucy confided in her mother. She said, "I was an excellent basketball player. To be on the team you had to wear shorts above the knees. Mama did what she had to do to get me money to buy those shorts without telling daddy; he did not know it." With money in hand for the shorts, Lucy was ready to play basketball.

"One night, I was playing basketball and looked up; I saw my daddy come into the gym. I just walked out of the gym. Daddy came up to me and said, 'Did you know God's looking at you.' I said mmhummm. He said that will not be happening again; so I had to quit. This was probably in the ninth grade, so there was not much sports activity for me after that."

Lucy's parents did not have regular jobs earning money, so they were dependent on the income they earned from the farm and milk cows. According to Aunt Lucille, Vady saved eggs and traded them to their neighbor Mrs. J.C. Fields for money. She said, "I took the egg money to buy my annual; I still have my annual today." The picture of Lucy's eighth grade class was from that Danville School annual.

EIGHTH GRADE

Reading from left to right:

First row	Second row	Third row
Billy Kirby	Faye Hall	Miss G. Glasgow
Bobby McCaghren	Jackuelyn Vest	Wade Holladay
William Depreast	Faye Kirby	Billy Jarrett
Betty Wallace	Mary Lois Maples	Prentiss Collins
Mildred Myers	Nenola Brown	Copeland Vest
Doris Long	Hilda Wilbanks	Charlie Callahan
Lucille Walker	Ruby Kirby	Denzil Burnett
Nell Tanner		James Depreast
		William Nethery

Katie Lucille lived in a very strict home controlled by her daddy. Because of his strong moral stand and his perception as an old timey Baptist preacher, he did not allow his children much freedom, especially his daughters. Dan Walker held a tight reign over his girls and did not allow them to make their own decisions about their night time activities before they were married. Dan tried to keep up with ever move his daughters made.

During Katie Lucille's school days, her activities were regulated by her father Dan Walker who was very strict. She was his baby girl, and he watched over her. Because of her father's religious beliefs, Katie Lucille did not have as many opportunities of independence as most of the other students in her class.

Not having unlimited freedom did not seem to be unacceptable to her because that was the only way she knew.

Dan Walker was so strict with Lucy that Ms. Vady would sometimes intervene in an attempt to allow Katie Lucille to enjoy school activities. Lucy's high school prom was coming up, and her mom agreed to let her go. Being the social butterfly she was, Lucy knew that she had to go to her junior-senior prom.

She said, "So on prom night in eleventh grade, mom got me this eyelet embroidery and made me a beautiful dress. So my friend Faye asked mother if I could spend the night with her. I was going to stay with her on the night of the prom so that I could go. I knew that Dan Walker would not let me go if he knew about it. Mama knew I was going to the prom, but daddy did not know; so Faye and I went to the prom," Lucy said. She should have known that her daddy would find out where she had gone, but she went anyway.

Dan questioned Miss Vady about where Lucy was. Vady did not lie to him. Katie Lucille said, "I and a friend were out there dancing and having a great time. I look up and there stands Mr. Walker. I knew my prom was over. So, I went over to daddy, and he took me home. He did not whip me. He did not say two words all the way home. There went my night. I was not mad at him. I just got over it."

Lucy's indifference toward her clothes and plow boots did not cause her any problems when it came to her school work. Although she did not get to participate in any extracurricular activities, Katie Lucille enjoyed school. "I did not have a lot of fun, but I made good grades. I made A's and B's all the time. I loved arithmetic." It appeared that Katie Lucille's siblings were also good at math.

"Faye Hall and Tobe White were some of my friends. One time, Tobe come up to the house, and dad was on the tractor. Tobe asked, 'Mr. Walker, can I take your daughter to the movie?' Daddy said, 'No, I do not think so, but you can go sit on the front porch.' So that was my date with Tobe White. That was my first date, and I was in the eleventh grade," stated Lucy.

Chapter Four

Soldier's Wife

When Katie Lucille (Lucy) Walker finished high school in 1951, the events of World War II had changed the role of women, and Lucy had witnessed that change. The working women of World War II had contributed to the United States having a successful and victorious outcome, and at the same time, had allowed women to enter the labor force. Although she had spent the first seventeen years of her life learning the role of a rural farmer's wife, Lucy was anxious to find a new role in the work force. Unlike her mother, Lucy would leave the farm and seek employment in the city.

Lucy would indeed find her first job in the City of Birmingham, Alabama, which was some eighty miles south of the cotton fields and farm where she had grown to adulthood. She had known for a long time that she did not want to spend the rest of her life on a farm. Katie Lucille had grandiose ideas about her future, and she dreamed of seeing the world.

Katie Lucille (Lucy) Walker

After her high school graduation, Katie Lucille made her first trip away from home and found her first job. She went to Hartselle and caught the Greyhound bus to Birmingham. She planned to spend time with Billie Sue, the daughter of her oldest sister Ida. Ida's daughter Billie Sue had moved south to Birmingham in Jefferson County, Alabama, to work. Lucy wanted to get away from home and get a job.

The visit with Billie Sue provided the opportunity Lucille was looking for. "When I was eighteen years old, I had gone to spend the week with Billie Sue in Bessemer, Alabama. I got a job as a waitress in a restaurant called the White Bell Cafe. One weekend, I was coming home on a Greyhound bus and got off at the Hartselle bus stop. I was waiting for someone to pick me up."

During her teenage years, Lucy and most of her friends in the rural country side had to depend on someone for transportation. In the 1950's, very few young high school graduates could afford to have their own car, and cell phones were not even invented. Katie Lucille was no different, and she had to find a ride.

"I was going to get word for my daddy to pick me up. I went into a café nearby to get me a hamburger and coke. This lady I knew there said, 'Hold on and do not call your dad yet.' She had somebody she wanted me to meet. We waited about ten minutes and then walked in this soldier. He was this real good looking Air Force man named Asa Walker."

Asa had joined the United States Army several years before his first introduction to Lucy. Their first meeting was in the country town of Hartselle that Lucy had first visited when she was a little girl riding in her dad's cotton wagon that was pulled by mules. Asa's folks lived in Hartselle, and he was on leave from his military assignment. Lucy's friend at the café first introduced her to Asa Francis Walker, Jr.

Lucy remembered that she and Asa talked for a long time in the café. "We walked from the café near the bus stop to the drug store. We got vanilla ice cream at the Hartselle Drug Store. His parents lived on Sparkman Street so we walked back to his house. After it started getting late, I told them that I had to go home. Asa's sister Nora had a car and said, 'I will take you home.'"

Nora took Lucy to the Dan Walker farm near Danville. Katie Lucille spent the weekend with her parents, but she did not tell them about meeting Nora's brother Asa. On Sunday afternoon, Katie Lucille went back to Bessemer to work, and she thought little about meeting Asa Walker. Meanwhile, Asa returned to his duty station in Washington, D.C.

"At the time of our first meeting, I was in love with T.H. Hardin. I would write him every day, but he failed to return my letters. I learned that he was seeing Dot Smith, who he eventually married." Katie Lucille never realized that being rejected by her first love would send her into a whirlwind romance that would eventually carry her around the world.

After Lucy found out that the love of her life was seeing another woman, she quit writing her old boyfriend. She decided to find someone new. She started thinking about the handsome Air Force soldier she had met in Hartselle. Katie Lucille wondered about the great adventures that her future would hold with a career military man.

Lucy stated, "I was ready for a new relationship and Asa in his soldier's uniform was impressive to me. Two days after we had met, Asa left and went back to Washington, D.C., where he was stationed. He was able to get the phone number where I worked by calling the cafe. After I went back to work in Bessemer, Asa called and we talked about our lives and his military service. Since I was living with my niece Billie Sue, I gave Asa the phone number where I was staying and my parents' home address; momma and daddy did not have a phone."

Since phone service was not available in rural areas, Lucy's parents depended on letters to hear from people outside their farm community. Katie Lucille did not expect to hear from her parents while she was in Bessemer, and she never expected to hear from a man she had just met who was living in Washington, D.C. To her surprise, she received a call from Asa Walker. They talked on the phone and wrote letters. They quickly became close friends.

"I worked two more weeks, and one day when I got to work, there sat Asa in the café in Bessemer, Alabama. We quickly developed a strong relationship, and he talked about getting married. Asa went back to Washington, D.C. After about three weeks went by, Asa came home on leave."

Asa was intent on living his life as a career soldier, and he wanted Katie Lucille to join him on his great adventure. Asa told Lucy how much he loved her, and how much he wanted to spent his life with her. After much consideration and prayer, Lucy felt she was ready to see the world and become a soldier's wife.

"While on leave, Asa came back to Bessemer at five AM on a Friday morning to pick me up. He said, 'Let's go get married;' I was hesitant but decided to go with Asa to Iuka, Mississippi, and get married. Since my sister Violene had gone to Iuka, Mississippi, to marry Willard Welborn, Iuka is where Asa and I decided to go," said Lucy.

Violene was Lucy's sister, and she had married Willard Welborn in Iuka, Mississippi, some four of years earlier. Violene and Willard moved to Gadsden, Alabama. Eventually, they had three sons: Danny, Sandy, and Ronnie. After Willard's untimely early death on September 17, 1954, at the age of twenty nine, Violene moved back to Morgan County, Alabama. Dan Walker built her a house on the family farm just a few yards south of his and Vady's home.

Lucy remembered that her sister Violene had no trouble getting married in Mississippi. Asa and Lucy were also ready to get married quickly, so they headed to Iuka, Mississippi. "I was just a poor country girl and did not have many clothes. All I had on was my waitress uniform, and I got in the car with Asa and headed to Mississippi."

It was obvious that Katie Lucille did not want her parents to think that she was leaving home by packing all of her clothes for five days of work in Bessemer; therefore, she only carried the clothes she need for work. When Lucy decided to go with Asa to get married, they stopped to buy clothes for her wedding, and Moulton, Alabama, was conveniently on the way to Mississippi. "When we went through Moulton, Asa stopped and bought me a two piece blue suit. He went to the jewelry store next door and bought a gold wedding band. I put the suit on at the store, and we headed toward Iuka, Mississippi."

Katie Lucille's plans had been blocked many times by her daddy. This time, she would not tell anyone of her pending marriage for fear that her daddy

Asa and Katie Lucille Walker

would try to stop it. Both she and Asa were anxious to become husband and wife. After a whirlwind romance, their marriage was the beginning of a new adventure for both.

"After we arrived in Iuka, Mississippi, we went to the preacher's house who had married Willard and Violene. The preacher's wife Emma played the wedding march, and the preacher conducted the wedding ceremony. We did not tell anybody that we were getting married."

Following her marriage to the career military man Asa Francis Walker, Jr., Lucy would keep her last name, and she became a soldier's wife. She would leave the cotton fields of North Alabama and follow her husband around the world. But now, it was time for Mrs. Katie Lucille (Lucy) Walker to go home and let her family know that she had married.

Marriage to Asa was a learning experience for Lucy. She was brought up living in a very devout Christian home with a father who was a Baptist preacher. Everything in life that was considered taboo, out of character, or in the least bit sinful by her father or mother was not allowed to be discussed in their home, especially sex.

Katie Lucille revealed a very personal note, "At that time we married, I did not know anything about being a wife and mother. I figured I would just learn as I went along. I didn't even know about my period until it happened. No one in my family talked about stuff like that." She had not even been told about having a period by her own mother.

Lucy was amazed how culture changed over the years. She lived to see television shows where women and men were in their underwear, regular advertisements about erectile dysfunction, and open discussions about gay/homosexual rights. Over the computer internet, people of all ages can see sexual acts and pornography. Sex is everywhere in today's society, but in the family and time that Katie Lucille (Lucy) Walker was growing up, even the word sex was not mentioned.

Following the wedding, Lucy and Asa immediately left Iuka, Mississippi, and they drove back to the Dan Walker's farm in Morgan County, Alabama. Lucy said, "It was late in the afternoon of April 18, 1952, when we got back to my parents' house in Danville. When we pull the car up to the house, daddy was on the front porch. I got out of the car and walked up to daddy. I laid the marriage license in his lap. Daddy did not say anything to me and looked at Asa and said, 'Have a seat.' I went in the house to tell mama."

Dan Walker was a man of few words, but he meant exactly what he said and backed it up with actions. He left no doubt in Asa's mind about his expectations of taking care of his youngest daughter after her marriage. "Mama and I decided to listen at the door to see what daddy was saying. He said, 'Let me tell you something son, if you ever decide you want to give her a whipping, you bring her home. If you ever decide you are tired of her, you better bring her home in good shape.' Daddy had not talked that much in months. He gave Asa all kind of instructions; he did not talk to anybody, but he sure talked to Asa."

Even though the rules of marriage to his baby daughter were spelled out very clearly by this hell fire and brimstone Baptist preacher, Dan Walker was very saddened that his youngest child and beloved baby daughter was about to leave her childhood home. After a few hours of visiting with Dan and Vady Walker, Mr. and Mrs. Asa Francis Walker, Jr. got in their car and went to Asa's parents' home in Hartselle, Alabama, where they stayed the night.

According to Katie Lucille, "Since momma and daddy knew that we would be leaving soon to report for military duty the next day, they came to Hartselle to visit with Asa and me at his parents' house and to eat some of the wedding cake. I was the last of their children to leave home. The occasion was sad for mamma and daddy. I had a hint of sadness, but I was happy to be Mrs. Asa Walker. The next day April 20, 1952, Asa and I started our journey together serving with the United States military. We went back to Washington, D.C., where Asa was stationed."

Katie Lucille did not take time to pack all of her clothes since she had to leave on short notice, but this would not be the only time in her life that she would leave on short notice without all of her clothes. "Two weeks later, we came back home so that I could pick up the rest of my clothes. When we came home on that leave, daddy was preaching at Friendship Church at Upshaw. Asa and I went to hear daddy preach. I was wearing a dress and wearing high heels. I also had on a white wide brimmed hat and had makeup on with bright red lipstick. That particular sermon, daddy preached about Jezebels; he preached me right under the pew!"

After getting her sermon on Jezebel and packing all her clothes, Lucy left the Alabama cotton fields and home of her youth never to return to the life of farming activities. After she and her husband return to military duty in Washington, D.C., Lucy immediately threw herself into the role of a soldier's wife. She was delighted with the opportunity to live in a big city a long way from the hard work in the cotton fields and farm life of the hill country of North Alabama.

Chapter Five

Military Life

Katie Lucille (Lucy) Walker said, "Asa was the only one of his family that went into military service." Asa was only seventeen years old when he joined the United States Army on February 13, 1946. The military career Asa chose was filled with hardships and new experiences which would also pose many problems for his future wife.

In the 1940s, not many jobs were available in Hartselle, Alabama, and none of those jobs offered world travel. So, Asa joined the United States Army in order to serve his country and see the world.

As a young man, he had enlisted in the United States Army at Fort McCellan, Alabama. He completed the tour of duty with the army on January 30, 1947, at Kelly Field, Texas. After completing a tour of duty with the army, Asa joined the United States Air Force. He signed up for another three year tour of duty. Asa had planned to see the world during the completion of a thirty year career in the military.

Aunt Lucille said, "Asa Francis Walker, Jr. was born on April 28, 1928; his father was Asa F. Walker, Sr. and his mother was Letha Bell Scott. His daddy was born around Haleyville in Winston County, Alabama; Asa, Jr. was born in rural Morgan County."

According to Aunt Lucille, "Asa, Sr. had six brothers and most were police officers in Winston County. I think I only met his whole family one time at a reunion. He did not visit and go around his family much. Asa, Jr. was close to his sister Nora than any of his other siblings. Nora died at the age of ninety four; our daughter Martha Jo was her caretaker. I think there were a lot of drunks in his family. Asa went in the military looking to better himself; he did not want to live in Hartselle, Alabama, all his life."

Asa Walker -5th from left Fort McCellan, Alabama, September 9, 1946

Asa F. Walker, Jr. made the decision at a very young age that he wanted to have a career in the United States military. He was a country boy from Hartselle, Alabama, who wanted to see the world and serve his country. During his some twenty four years with the military, he served in turbulent areas all over the world including two tours in Vietnam where he developed post traumatic stress disorder that probably contributed to his early retirement.

From the moment that Lucy said, "I do," she never dreamed that she would be meeting the man that she married in countries with names she had never heard. She would eventually follow Asa to United States outposts around the globe while he fulfilled his military obligations.

Lucy said, "Asa had already done one overseas tour when I met him; Asa and I married on April 18, 1952." During those years after their marriage, Asa was reassigned frequently by the military because of the turmoil and political unrest of the Cold War. The Cold War was an extended period of conflict between the United States and Communist nations that did not involve direct warfare.

During Asa's tour of duty in the 1950's and 1960's, political situations changed many times. As a result, more frequent moves were required by the Walker family. Each reassignment meant Lucy had to pack up all her worldly goods and move. On more than one occasion, the family did not stay in the same place for one year. Political unrest, base closing, and accidents interrupted the assignments of the Asa F. Walker, Jr. family. Those moves were in the days when anyone could drive up to the airport, walk in with ticket in hand, and board a plane for places unknown without question.

Their homes were associate with military bases, such as: Fort George G. Meade and Andrews Air Force Base, Maryland; Elmendorf Air Force Base, Anchorage, Alaska; Maxwell Air Force Base, Montgomery, Alabama; Shiroi Air Force Base, Japan; Anderson Air Force Base, Guam; Kelly and Lackland Air Force Base, Texas; Tempelhof Air Force Base, West Berlin, Germany; Chicksands Air Force Base, England; San Vito Air Force Base, Brindizi, Italy; and the list goes on.

On the day Katie Lucille Walker eloped with Asa, it never occurred to her that she was about to embark on a journey that would take her from the rural Alabama cotton fields to some of the most politically unstable places on earth. But like most young girls the future was not important. She was only living for the moment. She had graduated from high school, and she was ready to be with her military husband as a soldier's wife.

Chapter Six

April 1952-Andrews Air Force Base and Fort George G. Meade, Maryland, USA

After Katie Lucille (Lucy) Walker and Asa Francis Walker, Jr. were married on April 18, 1952, they stayed one day at Asa's family home on Sparkman Street in Hartselle, Alabama. This newly married couple arrived for military duty in Washington, D.C., on April 21, 1952.

Aunt Lucille said, "There was no honeymoon! One day after our marriage, we were on our way to Washington, D.C., in Asa's car. It was the biggest car that I had ever been in. We lived in Washington, D.C., but Asa worked at Fort George G. Mead, Maryland."

Katie's first military trip was with her husband to his assignment at Fort Meade, Maryland, only two days after they were married. That would be the last time she would accompanied him to his duty station. From that point forward, Lucille would be responsible for her own travel arrangements and finances to follow her husband to his military posts around the world. Little did she know that the scene of moving on short notice would be repeated over and over for the rest of his military career. She would meet Asa Walker in strange places in foreign countries for the next eighteen years; this would be the life of a soldier's wife.

Lucy Walker 1952
Washington, DC

62

The Fort Meade military installation was located in the northwestern portion of Anne Arundel County, Maryland, approximately halfway between the cities of Baltimore and Washington, D.C. The northwest boundary of the post is the Baltimore-Washington Parkway, and it was bounded on the south and southwest by the Patuxent Freeway. Fort Meade was named after a Union general in the United States Civil War by the name of George G. Meade. General Meade was the commander of the Army of the Potomac. Fort Meade, a United States Army installation which was utilized for military intelligence and national security from the 1950's through the 1970's, specialized as a radar station and control systems for air defense. Asa would be assigned to Fort Meade on more than one occasion during his military career.

Katie Lucille described her husband's duties, "Asa was a cryptographer with top secret security clearance in the United States Air Force; he sent and received messages. In addition, Asa also intercepted and decrypted enemy signals."

From the early days of their marriage, Lucy was the backbone of her family. She took responsibility for her husband as they embarked on his military career. As insecure and scared as she may have been taking on the role of a soldier's wife, she was willing to let go of her inhibitions and follow her dream.

Admittedly, Lucy missed the slow paced country life. There would be no more sitting on the porch at dusk listening to her dad read the Bible, watching the lightning bugs flash, and listening to the crickets chirping. Those familiar monotone sounds of a warm southern night would no longer lull her to sleep. At the age of eighteen, she never realized how much she would miss the life that she was determined to leave. But, she was ready for a new adventure, and she was excited about experiencing city life.

She did not realize that she had lived in such a small world; really a different kind of world. Her little world had been filled with a loving family and caring friends many of whom shared her hopes and dreams for a better life. Living in a big city would fulfill one of her dreams, but it would present a view of a different world: A world of indifference and strangers. Facing the unfamiliar would be a challenge even for such and outgoing young woman.

Katie Lucille found herself surrounded by different sounds and smells. Horns blowing, motors racing, lights flashing, and construction noises were everywhere in the big city. All those sounds seemed very foreign to a country girl who was gifted at picking cotton, and who had lived her life on an isolated farm in the Deep South.

Katie Lucille Walker, 1952, Washington, D.C.

The people she met on the streets seemed different. People were everywhere, but not one seemed to be aware of those who were around him. They were rushing from place to place, and they did not even take time to say "Hello."

One thing that helped the poor country girl overcome her anxiety of living in the big city was Asa's sister moving to Washington, D.C., to live with them after they had been there only a short time. Katie Lucille said, "Nora, Asa's sister, had gone through a divorce with a Petty who owned a drycleaners in Hartselle, Alabama. After her first divorce, she moved in with me and Asa in Washington D.C."

Since Katie Lucille did not know a lot about living in big cities, she was very thankful to have Nora living in their home. "We lived in a little apartment two blocks on the east side of the capital in Washington, D.C. I worked at Bell South Telephone Company as a long distance operator, and being southern, they would laugh at me because of my accent; therefore, they changed me to looking up addresses. I made one dollar and thirty cents per hour and that was big money."

Big money to Katie Lucille was more than five dollars per day; she never dreamed that she could make that much money in one hour. She loved her work and was very proud to have a job because jobs in rural Alabama were few and far from home. Lucy loved her job so much that she encouraged Nora to apply to the telephone company. After a few weeks, Katie Lucille managed to get Nora a job with the phone company. She said, "Nora got on at the phone company and worked for years."

Katie Lucille loved Nora and was extremely glad to have a home buddy to share her new adventure. "Nora was like a big sister; we did everything together. She was like a momma to me; Nora and I shopped a lot together. While in Washington, Nora married and divorced an Italian guy; she got alimony from him. They divorced because he would not take his boots off at the door, and she had white carpet. Nora lived in Washington about twenty five years."

Even though the newlywed couple had struggles and hardships they also had blessings. While living in Washington, D.C., two years after their marriage, Lucille and Asa had their first child who was born on April 2, 1954. They named their baby girl Martha Jo Walker. Becoming a mother was an amazing experience for Katie Lucille, but little did she know the added responsibility that she was facing. She was ready for the challenge of being a wife and mother.

As a soldier's wife there were some social and military obligations that Katie Lucille had to meet. Although she did not like to leave her baby to attend those functions, she reluctantly arranged for a baby sitter. Usually, Nora was anxious to take care of her niece. After making sure that her baby Martha Jo was safe and secure, Lucy would prepare for an evening out with her husband or to attend events at the non-commissioned officer club.

Of course, she had to have a fashionable cocktail dress, accessories, and shoes. Living on a tight budget meant Lucy had to make her own dresses, and she became an excellent seamstress. Although Lucy had no formal training as a seamstress, her mother had taught her to sew. Like her mother, Lucy made clothes for herself and her baby. She made sure that her baby Martha Jo was well dressed in the finest clothes she could make. Later in life, she would use her sewing skills to supplement her family income by making formal gowns and dresses for other young women.

Even though Lucy was raised in a small community where everyone knew everyone else, she welcomed strangers. She soon learned how important her ability to never meet a stranger would be to her husband's military career. She took on the challenge of entertaining military guests at her home. She was a southern girl at heart. When she moved to our nation's capital, she did not lose that "southern charm." She was an outgoing, friendly, young woman with warm welcoming smile. Moving from place to place did not hinder Lucy. She was always outgoing and seemed to be having lots of fun.

Although she was just an ordinary country girl from the North Alabama cotton fields, she could entertain with the best of them. Lucy by nature was a social butterfly with a twinkle in her eyes. So it was no surprise that she and Asa were frequently invited to dinner or parties. Many of those social events were hosted by officers and their wives. During this period of her life, Lucy seemed drawn to the "upper crust of military society."

No matter where they were stationed, Lucy was prepared to entertained new found friends and neighbors, especially high ranking officers, their wives, and families. Entertaining was not all about enjoying the food and the company of her guest. It provided her with an opportunity to convince the guests that her husband was an asset to the military. She knew that she could help Asa moved up the rank and get a higher pay check.

Lucy would have the post commander and his wife over for dinner. She made these great dinners to help her husband get promotions and find good favor from his commanding officers.

Lucy wanted Asa to be successful in his military career, and she was going to do everything in her power to help and promote her husband to his superiors. She strived to be the best and successful at everything she attempted. Helping her husband move up his military career ladder was just the way Lucy lived life as a soldier's wife.

Lucy and Asa eating with friends

Chapter Seven

April 1954-Elmendorf Air Force Base, Anchorage, Alaska, United States Territory

After Katie Lucille was with Asa for two years in Washington, D.C., he got assigned to Elmendorf Air Force Base at Anchorage, Alaska. Moving from the hot humid South to the cold frigid North presented a new set of challenges for Lucy. Living in Washington D.C., had made the transition a bit easier because she had learned to deal with cold weather and snow. However, it did not fully prepare her for the reality of months and months of snow, ice, and darkness with her baby daughter.

Lucy and Jo shortly after arriving in Alaska

Asa went to Alaska in April 1954; Lucy and the baby did not arrive until July. Asa's Alaskan assignment was immediately after the April 2, 1954, birth of his and Katie Lucille's first child, Martha Jo Walker.

Asa Walker and a fellow serviceman left Washington, D.C., and drove the ALCAN Highway to report for duty. Just a year later, Lucy would drive that same highway to return to Alabama with her baby girl.

At the time of Asa's assignment to Elmendorf in Alaska, Katie Lucille Walker drove with her baby Martha Jo from Washington, D.C., in their red Ford back home to Alabama. Katie Lucille said, "I packed everything up and came to Alabama. We stayed with momma and daddy until Jo was six weeks old."

After spending some two months at her rural home in North Alabama with her baby, Lucy was ready to join her husband in Alaska. For a short period, she was glad to return to the cotton fields and farm that had made her the woman she had grown to be, but it was time to continue the adventure with her soldier.

Lucy recalled her trip to Alaska, "Daddy drove us in his flatbed Dodge farm truck from Danville, Alabama, to Atlanta, Georgia, where Jo and I flew to Seattle, Washington. We got to Seattle in the late afternoon, and they said they did not have a flight. I talked to the captain of the mail plane to see if I could get a ride to Alaska. After he checked out the plane and was ready to fly, he allowed me and my baby to board his plane. I rode on a bag of mail with my baby from Seattle to Anchorage, Alaska." Upon her arrival, she was in awe of the breath taking scenery.

S/SGT. ASA F. WALKER, JR., of Hartselle has been joined in Anchorage, Alaska, where he is stationed with the U. S. Air Force by his tiny daughter, Martha Jo, and his wife, the former Lucille Walker of Danville. Mrs. Walker flew to Alaska to join her husband after he was transferred from Washington, D. C., where he had worked for two years at the Pentagon building. He has been in the Air Force for about eight years. Sgt. Walker is a foormer Morgan County High School student and is the son of Mr. and Mrs. A. F. Walker, Sr., of 208 Barclay Street. The above photo was snapped of Sgt. Walker and his daughter soon after her arrival in Alaska.

Hartselle Enquirer 1954

69

During their military assignment, Alaska was not yet a state, but it offered a new adventure for Asa and Lucy. A few years after they left Alaska, it was admitted as the forty ninth state of the United States on January 3, 1959.

Anchorage, located in the south central part of Alaska referred to as "The Banana Belt," was the largest city in the territory. The rather remote frontier town was growing, but it was still a small city in 1954. There were few paved roads. Often the dirt roads were muddy, rough, and some areas were almost impassable. Grocery stores as we know them were nonexistent, and most household goods were flown in from the lower forty eight. The area had few restaurants and movie theaters did not exist. Few people owned televisions and all programming was in black and white.

When Asa Walker got to Elmendorf Air Force Base in April 1954, the Alaskan base had assumed an increasing role in the defense of North America following World War II. The Cold War between the Soviet Union and United States had deteriorated into uncertain wartime relations between the two super power countries. The turbulent world situation in the 1950's caused a major buildup of air defense forces in Alaska. Eventually, the propeller-driven aircraft were replaced with jets and inceptor aircraft for defense of North America.

The United States Air Force built an extensive aircraft control and warning radar system with sites located throughout Alaska's interior and coastal regions. They built numerous support facilities around the territory to provide reliable communications to these isolated, distant, and rugged locations. Elmendorf served as the nerve center for all air defense operations in Alaska.

Asa Francis Walker worked for the United States Air Force Security Service. The security group Asa worked in was responsible for monitoring, collecting, and interpreting the intercepted intelligence signals of concern to the region during the Cold War. The Security Service had installed an antenna array as part of a worldwide network known collectively as "Iron Horse" in order to protect the United States. Eventually, Asa would work with the "Iron Horse" in at least two other worldwide locations.

Asa was a senior crypto operator while at Elmendorf Air Force Base. Air defense forces reached their zenith at Elmendorf in mid 1950's with almost two hundred fighter aircraft interceptor squadrons, and a total of eighteen aircraft controlled the operations. Elmendorf earned the motto "Top Cover of North America."

Katie Lucille said, "When Jo and I got to Alaska, Asa had us a nice apartment when we got there. His pay at that time was only one hundred and thirty dollars one time a month. It seemed that we were always on a tight budget and had very little money to survive the month."

Anchorage Alaska in 1954 was a far cry from the bustling city of Washington, D.C., and it would take Katie Lucille father away from the cotton fields of North Alabama. Supplies and people had to be flown into the town. Lucy and Jo arrived in Anchorage on July 4, 1954. Lucy said, "We got to Alaska on the fourth of July. Asa and I set on our little front porch and read the newspaper at eleven pm at night because it was still daylight."

The summer days were long, and it never got pitch black dark. However, the winter days were long, dark, and very little sunlight was seen during the twenty four hours. Winters in Alaska were brutal, and the winter of 1954 was no exception. Katie Lucille and her baby girl were not use to such cold. The frigid wind blew snow around the house where they lived and sidewalks had to be cleared. Avalanches and rock slides rolled down the mountains; banks of snow built up in their yard; cold weather lasted from August to May.

Lucy and Jo in the snow in Alaska

Lucy though ice skating would be fun, and the climate was certainly conducive to such an adventure. It was so cold in the winter that Asa laid out an ice rink in their backyard. The little ring was filled with water, and a couple of days later the yard ice rink was frozen solid. They were able to skate for short periods of time on mild days. Jo was only ten months old so she could not stay out for long. Lucy would dress Jo in her puffy snow suit and venture outside on pretty days. Since they did not own a car, Lucy had to walk where ever she went.

Alaska was the home of Mount McKinley, the highest peak in North America. In 2015, the mountain peak was renamed Denali. The mountain located in Denali National Park was visited by many people each year. Denali was some two hundred forty miles north of Anchorage, but it could be seen from great distances. Even in 1954 when Asa, Katie Lucille, and Martha Jo lived in Alaska, the huge beautiful mountains, Alaskan glaciers, and active volcanoes attracted tourist from all over the world to Alaska.

The beautiful coastline of the Pacific was unforgettable. Many areas were only accessible by plane, but the Walkers had an opportunity to explore the Alaskan wilderness. There were black bears, harbor seals, mountain goats, spawning salmon, sea otters, whales, porpoises, moose, sheep, grizzly bears, caribou, and American bald eagles. Lucy had never seen some of these animals in the wild.

The rugged land offered a new beginning for many including military families, but not for Katie Lucille and Asa. They would eventually find their way back to live near the cotton fields of their North Alabama home.

Situated along the south central Alaskan coast, Anchorage was prone to earthquakes. An earthquake struck while Asa, Lucy, and their baby Martha Jo were there. Lucy's little family survived this big Alaskan earthquake of 1954, but it etched a memory that she shared for the rest of her life.

Lucille said, "Asa was working swing shift, and he was home that day. He said, 'Get the baby and get under the bed.' There was an awful sound. We lived in a little block house when the earthquake happened. When it was all over, there was a crack down the wall and door from top to bottom." The earthquake damaged the area, but people just rebuilt knowing that a natural disaster would happen again and again.

Lucy said, "Hills that were there were there no longer. Trees were all gone. We lived by the railroad tracks, and it swallowed three railroad cars. The earth just opened up and swallowed those huge train cars."

Of all the states in the United States, Alaska is the most earthquake prone, and it is one of the most seismic active regions in the world. Alaska experiences a magnitude seven earthquake nearly every year, and on average every fourteen years, it has an earthquake of a magnitude of eight or greater.

Katie Lucille said, "After the earthquake damaged our house so bad that it could not be fixed, we moved into government quarters which were large brick buildings on the base like apartment buildings. The housing on the base was free as they were part of our benefits."

The main outdoor activities were hunting, hiking, and skiing. Asa was all about learning the sport of snow skiing. He would venture out with the guys for relaxation, and they would ski on the snow covered mountains. After mastering the slopes, Asa wanted to try the ski jump.

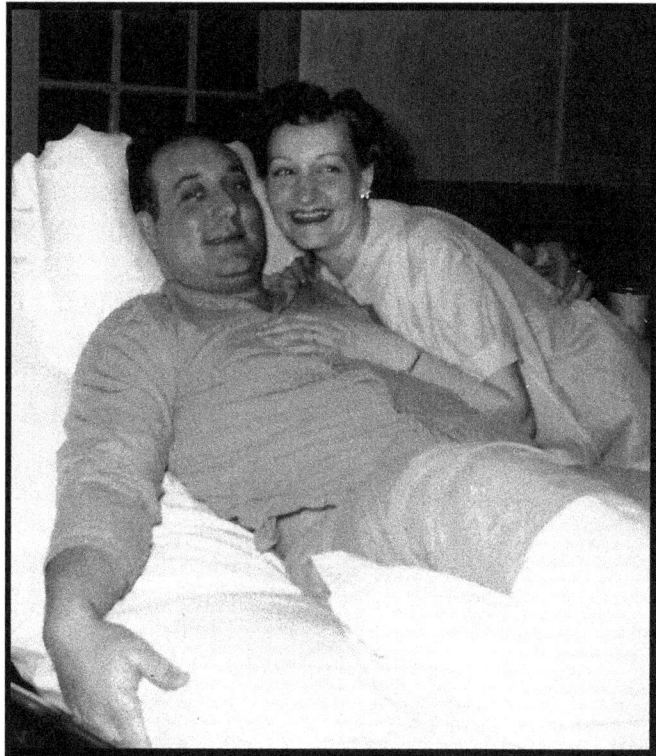

Asa and Lucy when he broke his leg

With his first attempt at the ski jump came the accident; one that would claim almost two years of his life and potentially end the military career that he had chosen.

Katie Lucille said, "Asa always wanted to go ski jumping on the snow covered slopes; it was so beautiful. So he and some guys went snow skiing. Asa missed the jump and broke his leg in thirteen places between his knee and ankle. Since we did not have a hospital at Elmendorf, they put him in the hospital at Fort Richardson Army Base about thirty miles from Anchorage."

After Asa's accident, the military sent him to Fort Richardson. Elmendorf Air Force Base and Fort Richardson were constructed in the United States Territory of Alaska in 1940. The two military bases were eventually merged to form Joint Base Elmendorf-Richardson. In 1954, Fort Richardson did not have the specialized medical facilities to correct Asa Walker's broken leg.

Lucy said, "We did not have a car so I got somebody to take me to see him. I went to see him, and his foot was turned wrong in the cast. I asked them what they were going to do about that. They said, 'We are going to send him where he can get some specialized help.' After my complaints about his medical care in Alaska, they sent Asa to Maxwell Air Force Base in Montgomery."

The military transferred Asa to a hospital at Maxwell Air Force Base in Montgomery, Alabama, where they had the technology to take care of his broken leg. After Asa left Alaska in April 1955, Lucy and baby Martha Jo were left to make the long arduous journey from Anchorage, Alaska, to Danville, Alabama, by themselves.

No longer a scared little country girl, but now a determined twenty two year old young mother, Lucy did what she had to do. She knew that she faced one of the biggest decisions she would ever have to make, but she could not think about anything but how to get home. Other decisions would have to wait for a few days. Her main concern was getting back to Alabama with her baby. She knew if she could just get to her mother on the farm in North Alabama that everything would be fine; then, she could figure out what to do about her severely injured husband.

Katie Lucille was left to finish clearing their quarters and find her own way back to Alabama to be with her husband. Since the military did not provide for travel for the spouse of an enlisted soldier, it fell on Lucy to provide the means and finances to get her and her baby back home to Alabama. She had to make all arrangement and pay for her own travel. Katie Lucille said, "I got the quarters cleaned in Alaska. I knew I had to get ready to move out because we would be told to clear quarters."

Regardless of the circumstance of her life, good or bad, Katie Lucille faced them with strength, courage, and determination. After hearing the doctor's report, she knew what she had to do. As devastated as she was, her inner strength took over. She began preparing to take care of her husband's paper work, clearing and cleaning her quarters, and preparing to move from Alaska to Montgomery, Alabama. She had to get needed supplies to take her baby on a long trip.

Shortly after Lucy said good bye to her husband who was being flown to Maxwell Air Force Base in Montgomery, Alabama, she went to pick up her baby. Lucy was left alone to prepare for the long, grueling journey back to Alabama. As a soldier's wife, she would be required to complete piles of paper work. She went from one office to another to fill out forms

Jo and Lucille Walker
Anchorage, Alaska 1955

and signing papers. "After I finished all the paper work and my duties at Elmendorf, I bought me a Chevrolet stick shift and drove from Alaska to Danville, Alabama with the baby." The long enduring trip from Alaska to

Alabama was made with a young baby, and Lucy was pregnant with her second child Mark.

With the task finally completed and all her worldly goods packed, Lucy and her baby daughter got into the Chevrolet and headed south. The trip from Anchorage was a long weary one for the young pregnant mother and her two year old daughter. She knew Anchorage, Alaska, was a little over four thousand miles from Morgan County, Alabama, but she never realized the time that the journey would take.

From Anchorage, Lucy drove the Alcan Highway through part of British Columbia, Canada. The highway was also known as the Alaska Highway, the Alaskan Highway, or the Alaska-Canadian Highway. The highway was constructed during World War II for connecting the contiguous United States to Alaska. It was completed in 1942, and the road was opened to the public in 1948 at a length of some seventeen hundred miles. In the spring of 1955, Katie Lucille Walker was pregnant and had her baby Martha Jo as she made the drive. The highway was a rough and challenging route, but Lucy was tougher than any road.

Wild animals such as deer, moose, bear, and wolves were seen roaming along the mountainous highways. Many sections of the road were isolated, unimproved, and in bad shape. There were not a lot of service stations, hotels, or rest stops along the way through Canada to the United States. After days on the road, Lucy and her baby daughter finally got back to Danville, Alabama. Lucy said, "My baby girl and I came back home to momma and dad in Alabama."

Chapter Eight

April 1955-Maxwell Air Force Base, Montgomery, Alabama, USA

After the skiing accident, the Air Force sent Asa to Montgomery, Alabama, in April 1955. He had to stay in Montgomery until September 1957. Katie Lucille Walker was determined to be with her whole healthy husband; therefore, she moved to Montgomery, Alabama. Lucy was a woman of great internal strength and determination. She was a soldier's wife who supported her husband.

Lucy Walker 1956
Danville, AL

The picture of Lucy was taken in 1956, and it shows her Chevrolet car that she drove from Anchorage, Alaska, to Danville, Alabama. The picture was taken at her parents' home some five miles south of Danville. Not only did Aunt Lucille travel to places all over the world to be with her military husband, she did the traveling by herself with her children in tow. She was unwavering in her loyalty to her husband and children. She made sure that she took care of all situations she faced without complaint or self pity.

Lucy said, "The military called and told me I needed to come down to Montgomery. They said I needed to sign some papers to amputate his leg at his thigh. I said, 'No, I aint signing any papers for y'all to cut off my husband's leg.'"

Lucy Walker

Even Katie Lucille's dad had questioned her decision to not allow doctors to take off Asa's leg, and she had to make a life or death decision. Dan Walker was concerned about his daughter knowing that she was pregnant with her second child. She told her dad how she felt about situation. Lucy had thoroughly considered the disability of her husband, but she wanted a whole man. She also knew that Asa wanted to complete his lifelong dream of having a thirty year career as a soldier.

Katie Lucille said, "Daddy asked me if I had really thought about the operation. I told him I was not going to live with two kids and a husband with no leg up to his groin. I said, 'I aint going to sign them papers.' He said, 'what if you lose him.' I said, 'I guess it will be God's will because I aint living with no half a man, I'm just not.' Dad did not say anything more about it."

Lucy made arrangements for Martha Jo to stay with her family, and she left to be with her injured husband. Based on the information she had been given at the hospital at Fort Richardson in Alaska, Lucy knew that she had a lot to figure out on the drive to Montgomery.

"So I went to Montgomery; I drove from momma and daddy's home in Danville to Montgomery by myself. I told them that they better get somebody down here to fix Asa's leg. I am not living with half a man. I am not signing papers for y'all to cut his leg off. I just walked out of the office. Asa and I had not really talked about what to do, but they did not even have it set right. I had time to really think this through while making the trip. I was fixing to have two kids, and I was not going to have a man that could not walk."

Not only was Katie Lucille stressed about the possibility of her husband having his leg cut off, but she was seven months pregnant with her second child. She was wondering how she would take care of two babies and a man that could not adequately provide for their family. At the same time in the back of her mind, she was determined to continue her great adventure with Asa's in his military career. She knew that if she agreed to amputation that her dream to see the world was over and Asa's dream to finish a military career would end prematurely; therefore, she made the heart wrenching decision to not sign any papers to have Asa's leg removed.

"In May 1955 when I got to the hospital in Montgomery, they said, 'You must sign these papers.' I said, 'I am not signing anything. I am fixing to have another baby in two months and you just better get somebody here to fix his leg.' The doctor said it would be in my best interest to sign the papers. I said, I think my judgment is better than yours" as Katie Lucille expressed her courage and unrelenting decision. The military finally realized that Asa's leg had to be repaired as best they could; therefore, bone specialists were called and ordered to surgically fix the broken leg.

Lucy knew how bad her husband wanted to be in the military, and she was one hundred percent behind his career decision to stay thirty years in the United States Air Force. Her actions and determination that Asa keep his leg saved his military career. Lucy also had personal reasons for her decision to make sure that Asa had two legs. Her courage saved a military career and probably their marriage.

Lucy said, "After a long hassle, they did get a doctor that did bone work. They put Asa on this board and would put a board on top of him so they could roll him over. Asa stayed at Maxwell about two years. They had to insert a rod and then take it out. When he got out of the hospital, we moved to an apartment in Montgomery."

Lucy's unwavering determination had pay off for Asa. He got to keep his leg that had been broken in thirteen places. After a long hospital stay, he was ready to continue his military duties. With the move into the new apartment completed and his leg on the mend, Asa began thinking about his family in Hartselle. Although it was just a short time before the baby was due, Asa and Lucy decided to make a trip to their parents' homes in North Alabama to celebrate the Fourth of July holiday with their family, relatives, and friends.

Jo, Lucy, and Mark in Montgomery, AL

"We came to Hartselle for the Fourth of July in 1955, and I went into labor. I said, 'I think I am about to have this baby.' Asa said, 'You cannot have this baby; we are in Hartselle.' While I was at the emergency room signing papers, I look over and who do I see sitting there was Tobe White, my first boyfriend and old school buddy."

Lucy said, "Asa's sister-in-law was head nurse there. I said, 'You better get me back there because I am going to have this baby.' I had Mark while we were in Hartselle for vacation. We went to Asa's parents the next morning, and the next day, we headed back to Montgomery."

While they were home on leave from Maxwell Air Force Base in Montgomery, Alabama, Mark Steven Walker was born July 9, 1955, in Hartselle, Alabama. Katie Lucille Walker was one tough lady. Two days after having her second child, they were on their way back to Montgomery, Alabama.

Mark was only one year old when Lucy became pregnant with her third child. Before the family left Montgomery, Katie Lucille gave birth to her third child Asa Lynn Walker on April 6, 1957, at Maxwell Air Force Base in Montgomery, Alabama.

Dan Walker Family when Lucy was home on military leave
Vady, Dan, Roy, Thurman, Paul, Oliver
Kenneth, Ida, Lodean, Violine, Lucy, Brady

Within a few months after the birth of Mark, Asa received his orders to report to Shiroi Air Force Base in Japan. Prior to Asa being sent to Japan, the family came home on leave. Since this was the first time that Katie Lucille Walker was on military leave in Alabama after marrying Asa, her Walker folks started having family reunions so that she could visit with all her brothers, sisters, in-laws, nieces, and nephews. The first gathering was at her parents' home south of Danville, Alabama. All of Lucy's immediate family members were expected to be at Dan Walker's house which was the designated site of the reunion.

Each brother and sister was also expected to bring enough food to feed themselves, their spouse, and children. All the food was set on the big table where the men got to fill their plates first. The women had second choice to eat and feed their babies. The children who were old enough to take care of themselves were the last that were allowed to come to the table.

Some of the young children were lucky to wind up with a chicken neck or wing on their plate, but most of the time, all the chicken was already gone. Since the Walker men got to eat first, the children would wait until they got the order from their mothers to go to the table to eat what the men had left. The choice pieces of meat and vegetables were gone by the time the kids got to the table to eat.

During the times Katie Lucille was home on leave, the Walker sisters, their mother Vady, and nieces got together to make crepe paper flowers to put on loved ones graves. In the 1950's and 1960's, plastic flowers were not readily available. If artificial flowers could be found, the family did not have the money to buy the floral arrangements. Therefore, the ladies and girls would get together to make crepe paper flowers for cemetery decorations.

The Walker women made their floral designs using primarily crepe paper and other easily found materials. The flowers were made by cutting pedals out of the crepe paper then twisting each one individually to the end of a piece of wire. The crepe paper petals were secured to the wire with a quilting thread. Each flower, held by the wire stem, was dipped in hot liquid bees wax; it was then stood upright in a mason jar to dry. The thin wax coating on the paper flowers would allow them to withstand changes in the weather for an extended period.

Katie Lucille loved making flower arrangements and would participate in the activity every time she was home on leave for a week or more. She continued to help her mother Vady make flora designs for graves of relatives even after the plastic flowers were readily available.

After the women completed their grave decorations, they would take them to Friendship Cemetery at Upshaw and Mount Vernon West Cemetery just northeast of Addison in Cullman County. Vady's mother and daddy were buried at Mount Vernon, and her little children and other relatives were buried at Upshaw.

While home on leave, Katie Lucille and other family members would visit and decorate the graves of loved ones. It was on one of these family visits that Lucy informed her parents that Asa had received orders to go to Japan. Montgomery, Alabama had seemed a long way from home, but Lucy and the children had made several visits to her parents in Danville while Asa was stationed at Maxwell. But, she knew that future visits would be only during Asa's three year reassignments.

After two years in Alabama at Maxwell Air Force Base, Asa received orders for Japan. His tour of duty in Japan would be the first foreign country that Katie Lucille and her three children would live. The members of her family hated to see Lucy and her children move that far away from home.

Dan, Vady, and her siblings knew that it would be some three years before they would see Katie Lucille and her children because that distance would restrict her travel. The cost of the airfare would be too great, and the trouble of moving that distance with children would be too much trouble. A return trip home would require too much effort unless it was an absolute emergency. The only means of staying in touch would be by written letters; none of Lucy's immediate family owned telephones.

Chapter Nine

September 1957-Shiroi Air Force Base, Japan

When Asa Walker was released from the hospital in Montgomery, Alabama, he was assigned to a three year tour of duty at Shiroi Air Force Base, Japan. From Montgomery, Alabama, he flew straight to Tokyo, Japan, in September 1957. The military did not make arrangements to send Asa's wife and his three young children on the long flight from the United States to Japan. That meant that Lucy would have to make the arrangements for the trip. Lucy and her three young babies were responsible for paying and finding their way to Asa in Japan.

When Asa received his orders to Japan, Katie Lucille was elated. She could hardly wait to move her family to Japan. She wanted her children to have the experience of living abroad; and of course, she had always wanted to see the world.

Her parents were not as excited, and she was reminded of December 7, 1941, the day that would "Live in Infamy." Although the war had been over for almost ten years, some unanswered questions still loomed. Lucy knew her history, and she was made aware of the political situation involving the Japanese.

On December 7, 1941, Japan attacked the United States at Pearl Harbor in Hawaii. Thus, the United States joined the Allies and entered World War II in full force. Four long, grueling years of fighting the Japanese in the Pacific followed. Japan was finally defeated in World War II after the United States planes dropped atomic bombs on two Japanese cities: Hiroshima and Nagasaki.

On September 2, 1945, Japan surrendered and World War II ended. Following the end of World War II, the Allied forces under the leadership and command of United States General Douglas McArthur occupied Japan. The occupation had two major goals; one was to disarm and demilitarize the Japanese, and the other was to establish a democratic form of government in Japan.

With the goals reached and a peace treaty signed, the Allied occupation of Japan ended in 1952. Although occupation had ended, the United States military troops remained because the United States-Japan Security Treaty of 1951 permitted the United States to build and man military bases in Japan. Many Japanese became infuriated over the continued presence of the United States military, and as a result, tensions and suspicions grew.

Now, Katie Lucille grew a bit more apprehensive. She had no idea of how an American family would be received by the proud Japanese people since their country had suffered such a humiliating defeat at the end of World War II. In spite of that, her determination to support her husband in his chosen career dictated her actions.

In the midst of the escalating political unrest with the Japanese, Katie Lucille and her three children traveled to the *"Land of the Rising Sun."* She said, "Asa went ahead of us. At this time, Asa and I had three children that were Martha Jo, Mark, and Asa Lynn. Martha Jo was the oldest, and she was only four years old. Then eleven years later, I had Cynthia and Roger. My three kids and I went from Hartselle on the train. We rode the train from Alabama to Virginia then got on a plane and ended up in Tokyo, Japan."

Lucy had two small baby boys in diapers and a young daughter to ride on a train for several hours. Then she had to manage the kids on a fourteen to sixteen hour flight across the ocean to Japan. Again Lucy was going to be with her husband in a foreign land with no one to help or accompany her.

Acceptance in a new community was not always easy. It had to be earned, and even for an outgoing southern country girl like Lucy that was sometimes challenging. Again and again, she would find herself ensnared by the language barrier, but she did not let language prevent her from getting to know people and becoming part of her new community. In spite of the language barrier, Lucy would find a way to communicate. Still, cultivating new friendships took time and with small children there was not much spare time to socialize.

Uneasy and anxious, Lucy had no idea what to expect on her arrival in Japan, but she did not know fear; fear would not direct her actions. She knew that moving to Japan meant another new set of challenges awaited. She realized that there would be cultural differences, but she had not really thought about the major challenge she was about to face. Upon her arrival in Japan, Lucy quickly became aware that the language barrier would definitely be her major obstacle.

She said, "After the kids and I got to the Tokyo airport, there were hundreds of strange people. We had never been outside the United States and were all of a sudden in a very strange country with very strange people, and, I could not speak their language. By the time we got into the airport, my kids were thirsty and wanted some water. This kind little Japanese lady came up and led us to some water; she said, 'It is called mesew.' After a while of waiting, I saw Asa come in the airport where I was waiting with the kids." From the Tokyo airport, the family traveled to Shiroi, a small Japanese village near the base where Asa worked.

Not only was it farther from Alabama than any other duty station, but people spoke an entirely different language. Learning a foreign language was not as difficult for Martha Jo as it was for her mother. Lucy was able to pick up a few necessary phrases and words, but she never mastered the Japanese language. Martha Jo said, "I spoke Japanese; I learned to speak Japanese in six to eight weeks.

Even though Lucy faced new challenges with cultural changes, different customs, and language barriers by moving to Japan, she took it all in stride. She introduced her children to this diverse Japanese society as best she could. She enrolled her young daughter Martha Jo in dance classes. Jo said, "I wore kimono which was a beaded Japanese dress with a big bow in back. The shoes I wore were like ballerina slippers. I was the only blond girl in the Japanese dances. I was on the front row in dance class so that my mother and I could be seen by the Japanese people."

Lucille Walker Family December 29, 1957

The family lived in Shiroi which was a Japanese village created within Chiba Prefecture district on April 1, 1885. It was not classified as a town until September 1, 1964. During the time Asa Walker was stationed at the base, it was a rural agricultural area noted for its fruit growing. The major fruit crops were kiwi, grapes, and the famous nashi pears. Shortly after World War II, Shiroi Air Force Base was utilized as a United States military base. On November 1, 1958, the security group was moved from the Shiroi Air Force Base to the Wheeler Air Force Base in Hawaii, but Asa was assigned to Anderson Air Force Base in Guam.

Lucy and Asa Lynn
Japan 1958

Lucy said, "Shiroi Air Force Base was nothing big. We did not live on base, but rented a house. We lived off base in the mayor's rental house which had dirt (red clay) floors. At Shiroi, we lived in the community of Lutsamay. Asa got in with some construction people after we were there a while, and we got some wood floors. We did not have hot water. Asa got a five gallon bucket, and he put it up in the corner of one of the rooms ran pipes up there so we could build a fire under it to have hot water."

Since labor was very cheap and there was no minimum wage in Japan, Asa hired a maid and baby sitter to help Katie Lucille. The Japanese people, especially women, were willing to work for extremely low pay. Asa paid a Japanese woman by the name of Ukeyco to help Lucy take care of their children Martha Jo, Mark, and Asa Lynn. She also helped Lucy cook the meals and clean the house for the Walker family.

Most of the houses in the village were small, one story structures that were separated from the neighbors by bamboo fences. The mayor's family lived in the house next to Asa and Lucy's home.

Asa Lynn Walker and Ukeyco
September 28, 1958, Japan

"The mayor's family lived in the house that was next to ours. There was a bath house at the mayor's home and the Japanese family would all take a bath together. One night Asa was working, and I kept hearing a noise going oosh oosh. I finally get the courage to open the door, and I see the Mayor naked as a jaybird with a towel going back and forth saying oosh oosh. He had his towel drying off going oosh oosh," recalled Katie Lucille.

"I slammed the door shut, locked it, and thought I would get me a nail; I will nail the door shut." But, Lucy and her children had nothing to fear. The Japanese neighbors were very friendly and welcoming to Katie Lucille's family. The Japanese just had much different customs than those of a country girl from the cotton fields of North Alabama. Lucy was not accustomed to seeing members of the same family bathe together.

Lucy said, "The mayor had a porch on his house and on the porch was a rice pot. They had a fire going all the time, day and night, and they had rice all the time. Rice is what they ate most of the time."

"We didn't have a porch. We ate what we could. We lived on one hundred and thirty dollars a month. Our electric bill was thirty dollars, and we got paid the first of the month. By the end of the month, we did good to have pinto beans and cornbread if I was careful with the meal."

Although food was sometimes in short supply, Lucy managed to see that her family did not go hungry. Living in a foreign country gave Lucy an opportunity to learn more about some strange and exotic foods, but she never lost her taste for good old southern foods such as fried chicken and potatoes.

The circumstances of life were not easy for military wives and their families. Lucy had to contend with the same problems and issues that other military wives faced on a daily basis. Soldiers were paid once a month, so managing finances always seemed to be an issue. With almost every dollar earmarked for necessary living expenses there was little disposable income. Having money for food was one of Lucy's main goals. Extras like new clothes had to be planned well in advance.

Asa was stationed at the Shiroi Air Force Base, Japan until the base was closed in October 1959. After the base closed, Katie Lucille packed up all the family's belongings, and she made arrangements for her family to go to their new assignment on the Island of Guam. Katie Lucille said, "We stayed in Japan until November 1959. The Japanese people were nice and treated us very well."

When the Shiroi Air Force Base in Japan was closed, Asa Walker was assigned to duty at the Anderson Air Force Base in Guam to complete the three year tour. As always, Aunt Lucille prepared to leave their Japanese home. As an outgoing social butterfly who never met a stranger, Katie Lucille sadly said good bye to her Japanese friends and neighbors.

Chapter Ten

November 1959-Anderson Air Force Base, Guam

Getting ready to leave Japan for Guam, Katie Lucille packed up all the family's belongings by herself. She got her children and all their household possessions ready for the move. Lucy had their furniture and other belongings loaded on a ship.

She did the best she could to find a way to be with her husband in his new assignment on the Island of Guam. After checking various modes of transportation, a vegetable supply plane appeared to be the cheapest and most efficient way to travel. Katie Lucille was able to get permission from the pilot for herself and her children to fly on the supply plane. She said, "We rode a supply plane from Tokyo, Japan, to Guam. The kids and I had to sit on vegetable crates filled with lettuce on our way to Guam. On the plane, I had only one suitcase and my three children. We went to Guam where Asa could complete his tour of duty after the Shiroi base closed."

Katie Lucille Walker arranged for all the household furnishing to be sent by ship from Japan to Guam. When the ship carrying all her worldly goods sailed, Lucy never dreamed it would not make port in Guam. Upon arriving on the beautiful Island of Guam, Lucy found out the ship carrying all her family's possessions including their clothes had sunk.

After arriving in Guam, all the family had was the sole contents of that one suitcase. Katie Lucille's daughter Martha Jo said, "All our belongings were lost when the ship bringing our furnishings sank. All our stuff was on the ship that sank while making the voyage to Guam."

Katie Lucille and her family were on an island completely surrounded by the Pacific Ocean. The serene waters along the island's beaches soon made the loss seem less important. Just being able to relax on the sandy shores of the island was something she had never imagined doing. Lucy, Martha Jo, Mark, and Asa Lynn found time to frolic on the undisturbed beaches and play in the pristine waters.

Katie Lucille and her children made several shore excursions to the many historical places and beautiful sights on Guam that were seldom seen by the average tourist. Locals on the island gave them directions for exploring the places unknown to the occasional visitors and travelers. Much leisure time provided unique opportunities to experience local markets, visit historic sites, and simply relax on the beautiful sandy beaches.

Guam is on a straight line between and about three fourths of the way to the Philippines from Hawaii. Much of Guam had been destroyed during World War II by fighting between the United States and Japan. The Japanese took the island from the United States after the bombing of Pearl Harbor and controlled the area for two and one half years during World War II before it was recaptured. In isolated areas on surrounding islands, some Japanese soldiers never got word the war was over until years later.

The northern part of the island was a flat limestone plateau and had the villages of Yigo and Dedeo. Dedeo was Guam's most populous village. The Anderson air base was about 30 miles from the Naval Base Guam. The two United States military bases were located on opposite ends of the island.

Asa worked on the Anderson Air Force Base which was located about four miles northeast of Yigo in the United States Territory of Guam. The island was liberated from the Japanese by the United States Marine Corps on July 21, 1944. An area on the remote Island of Guam was cleared for an airfield during World War II with the Anderson airstrip and base established on December 3, 1944. The base was named for Brigadier General James Roy Anderson (1904-1945) who was killed in a crash of his B-24 Liberator aircraft on February 26, 1945.

When Lucy and her children arrived on the island in 1959, the country was still in the process of rebuilding. Quonset huts left behind after World War II became homes for the active duty airmen following the war. Lucy and her family lived in a converted Quonset hut that was built by soldiers during World War II. The hut consists of an arch frame with metal siding. Martha Jo said, "While we were in Guam, we lived in a Quonset hut off base. Close to our living quarters was the Pacific Coast. Our home had half walls which separated the living area. The home had no corners except at the ends which had gates."

At the time Asa was working on the base, Guam was a territory of the United States; however, Lucy and her family were still living in a foreign country and a different culture. By 1950 the people of Guam were United States citizens. During the 1960's, the United States President appointed the governor of Guam.

Many of the people spoke English because of the large number of military families that lived in Guam. The native people of Guam spoke Chamorro which was their aboriginal language. Martha Jo said, "I learned to speak the language in Guam in about six weeks. Within some six to eight weeks, I could converse in the native language where we lived. While we were in Guam, I was not old enough to go to school." Today, English and Chamorro are the official languages of Guam; English is the dominate language.

Guam was a unique area where ancient ways of Pacific island life were still practiced. Many small villages still carried on their old ways of life; many of the islanders farmed. The island was a rather idyllic place with a lush landscape and pristine waters. Guam was a distinctive mix of primitive and modern with warm blue-green waters and miles of sandy beaches and coral reefs. Dense vegetation spread throughout the jungle of Guam; lush green forest, rocky terrain, hills, mountains, natural setting palm and banana trees, volcanic lakes, thriving bamboo forest, an undergrowth of ferns, and wild flowering plants covered the island.

Typhoons and earthquakes were typical natural disasters of the area, but Lucy did not mention experiencing an earthquake like the one she faced while living in Alaska. However, in 1962, while Lucy and her family were living in England, Guam was hit by a major typhoon that destroyed many of the buildings and left the land desolate again.

Living in Guam for Lucy's family was like being on an extended vacation. The mild climate was conducive to year around beach living. The family had no telephones, televisions, or computers; so, they spent most of the time outside. Katie Lucille and her children roamed the beaches looking for seashells and swam in the clear water of the Pacific; an occasional ship could be seen across the horizon.

It was in this setting that Katie Lucille realized that her life was far from the cotton fields of Morgan Country, Alabama, and it was days before a letter could be delivered. Lucy did not have a telephone in Guam and words from home were rare. She was a long way from the rules of her daddy's home. So she lived as an islander and sported the latest bikinis. This very scanty piece of clothing would never have been acceptable to Dan Walker, but it was the way of the life on the island.

Lucy and her three children walked along the sea shore, visited sites such as corals reefs and enjoyed breathtaking views of the Pacific Ocean. Up close encounters with sea life were ordinary occurrences.

Lucy in her latest swim suit

They enjoyed traditional foods like grilled shrimp, fresh pineapple, bananas, and coconuts. Life was a bit calmer there than it had been at Asa's other duty stations. The year and half in Guam passed rather rapidly and without a major incident.

Martha Jo said, "We had a house boy in Guam that helped with taking care and watching us kids. He also did some work around the house and in the yard. We would go to the beach and pick up sea shells; it was hot sandy beautiful beach. The island had lots of pineapples and bananas."

After the World War II, Guam served as a collection point for surplus war materials of the Pacific campaign. At the time Asa F. Walker, Jr. was working on the Island of Guam during the fall of 1959, he had no idea that ten years later Guam would be a major base for the air campaign in the Vietnam War where he would spend two years of duty. While Asa served in the Vietnam War, aircraft from the Anderson Air Force Base on Guam began regular bombing campaigns from June 1965 until 1973. Presently, the base provides support to aircraft and bomber crews deploying overseas in Europe, Southwest Asia, and the Pacific.

Today, the Island of Guam is a modern United States Territory with many luxury hotels and resorts; high-end shopping centers and outlets; bustling nightlife with bars, karaoke joints, and dance clubs. The shorelines of the island have plentiful beaches with water sports like parasailing, kite boarding, boating, and personal watercraft. At the museums, historic areas of World War II, cultural villages, and craft places, one can find woven items, rope, sea salt, coconut candy and coconut oil. Guam is much different today than when Katie Lucille Walker and her family spent one and one half years on the island in 1959 and 1960.

Chapter Eleven

June 1960-Kelly Air Force Base, San Antonio, Texas, USA

USA&USAFRIS, 106 Philipson Bldg, Gadsden, Ala, 30 Mar 49
Reenlisted this date by the undersigned for a period of
three (3) years   USAF Unasgd.

Edward L. McCoy
EDWARD L. McCOY
Captain, USAF
Reenlisting Officer

Army of the United States

Honorable Discharge

This is to certify that

ASA F WALKER   JR

Private   RA14 213 168   4505th AAF Base Unit

Army of the United States

is hereby Honorably Discharged from the military
service of the United States of America.

This certificate is awarded as a testimonial of Honest
and Faithful Service to this country.

Given at   Kelly Field Texas

Date   30 January 1947

PRENTIST C JONES
Major Air Corps

During his military career, Asa Francis Walker, Jr. was assigned to Kelley Air Force Base near San Antonio, Texas, on three occasions. When he was seventeen years old, Asa enlisted in the Army Air Corp. During his first tour of duty, he was stationed at Kelly Field, Texas. Asa's first tour of duty at Kelly was some five years before he and Katie Lucille Walker had met. During his initial tour, Asa was a single man, and he lived on base in the barracks. At the end of his first enlistment, Asa was discharge from the United States Army at Kelly Field on January 30, 1947.

Kelly Air Force Base is located near the southwestern edge of San Antonio, Texas. Prior to its closing in 2001, the base was the oldest operating base of the United States Air Force. The site was selected for Kelly Air Force Base in November 1916. The base was named in 1947 after Lieutenant George E. Kelly who was killed in a military aircraft crash at Fort Sam Houston on May 10, 1911. Many combat airmen of World War II received their training and wings at Kelly Field.

During Asa's second tour of duty at Kelly Air Force Base, he and his wife Katie Lucille were in Texas for some eleven months from June 1960 to April 1961. The family lived in a very arid region of mostly scrub brush. Lucy said, "We lived on Whitfield Road which was on the south side of San Antonio in a small Jim Walter style frame house without any porches."

Asa and Katie Lucille had planned to make their home in Texas, and they bought a home in San Antonio. After living in their home less than a year, Asa was issued new orders to Germany. Lucy said, "When we left Texas for West Berlin, Germany, we sold our house in San Antonio."

During the family's first stay in Texas, Asa's salary was barely enough to adequately support the family. Katie Lucille recalled, "Asa did not make much money and keeping food on the table by the end of the month was a continuous struggle."

During Asa's second tour of duty at San Antonio, Texas, his and Lucy's young daughter Martha Jo started school. Martha Jo said, "I started school while we were at Kelly Air Force Base. The school was a public school on south side of San Antonio. We lived in a small frame house that did not have a porch on the front or back. Rose bushes were planted around the house."

Jo continued, "One day I was out playing and though I saw a rope lying at the base of one of the rose bushes. As I started to pick up the rope, my mother stopped me with a scream. The object was not a rope. It was a huge rattlesnake coiled up near the base of the rose bush. Rattlesnakes were always coming in our yard and hiding around the house. This is a memory that sticks out in my mind while in Texas for daddy's second tour of duty there."

Even though his assignment papers were Kelly Air Force Base, Asa F. Walker, Jr. actually worked on the Lackland Air Force Base which was created from a section of Kelly Field in 1942. Construction of Lackland began on June 15, 1941. The base was named after Brigadier General Frank Lackland. In late 1951, the air defense command selected Lackland Air Force Base as one of the twenty-eight radar stations built as part of a permanent radar surveillance network. Asa worked primarily in military surveillance and intelligence gathering while at Lackland.

The Lackland Air Force Base was just across the road from the frame house from where Katie Lucille's family lived. The proximity of his work site to his house in made it very convenient for Asa to go to work, and it gave Asa the opportunity to spent a great deal of his time at home with Lucy and the kids. Martha Jo said, "When we were in Texas on daddy's tour of duty there for some ten months, mother did not work a public job. She spent most of her time taking care of us kids."

While on any of the many military facilities where they were stationed, Lucy's family usually attended the protestant church services at that particular base. Martha Jo said, "The military worship services were usually well organized on Sunday morning with services being at separate times; Baptist services were from nine to ten o'clock; Methodist services were from 10:10 to 11:10; Catholic services were 12 noon to 1:00 pm; and, Lutheran services were 1:00 pm until 2:00 pm. All base church services stayed on schedule. The worship and sermon was not the experience that we were use to in North Alabama."

Jo continued, "We sometimes went to church on the base. Military church was all formal, and the spirit of the Lord did not move in the church, like it did when I got to go to church with Aunt Lodean. I would see that little aunt of mine get the spirit and shout, clap, and move like I had never seen. The first time I saw it, I was a little scared, but I finally found out that was how it should be in a spirit filled church."

Years later, Katie Lucille and her daughters, Martha Jo and Cynthia, would become members of that same spirit filled church in North Alabama that Lucy's sister Lodean Walker Prater attended. They too would become spirit filled Christians like those that Martha Jo had remembered as a young girl while attending church with her Aunt Lodean.

While Asa was serving his second tour of duty at Kelly Air Force Base, he received orders to go to Tempelhof Air Force Base in West Berlin, Germany. During the time of his assignment, the Cold War between the United States and the Soviet Union was heating up and Berlin was the hot spot of contention in relations between the two countries.

Lodean Walker Prater and Katie Lucille Walker

Chapter Twelve

April 1961-Tempelhof Air Force Base, West Berlin, Germany

Tempelhof Central Airport was an airfield in West Berlin, Germany, utilized by the United States Air Force between 1945 and 1994. The base was located in the northern part of Tempelhof district of Berlin about two miles from the center of the city. In April 1961, Asa Francis Walker, Jr. worked at Tempelhof, and his family lived in a house that was adjacent to the boundary between East and West Berlin, Germany.

Tempelhof was a historic area that was used by King Fredrick William I in 1721, and it remained a parade ground until 1918. The area was also utilized as a demonstration area for balloons, airships, and aircraft, including flights by Orville Wright and his flying machine. In 1936, Germany opened the Tempelhof Airport on the site; however, they did not use the airport during World War II except for emergency purposes.

In April 1945, the airfield was captured by Russian forces of the Soviet Union; later in July 1945, it was turned over to the United States as part of the zones they occupied in West Berlin. In 1947, Tempelhof became a United States Air Force base. Between June 20, 1948, and September 30, 1949, Soviet troops closed off all roads into West Berlin causing Tempelhof to be utilized to transport tons of supplies known as the Berlin Airlift into the isolated city.

On February 28, 1958, the United States Air Force renamed the airfield Tempelhof Central Airport, and it was used primarily by United States military air traffic until the end of the Cold War. After the airport, air field, and base came under control of the United States, Asa and his family were assigned to a three year tour of duty at Tempelhof.

As usual, Asa had to report to his new assignment in Berlin, Germany. He left Katie Lucille to pack all the family's belongings in Texas. She had make travel arrangements to be with her husband. Upon completing all the necessary paper work and completing travel schedules, Lucy decided to return to Alabama with her children for a visit with her family prior to leaving for West Berlin, Germany.

After a visit with relatives in Alabama, Katie Lucille Walker and her children went to Germany in April 1961 where her husband Asa was stationed at Tempelhof Air Force Base in West Berlin. They lived off base while Asa worked with the security forces in top secret missions of the Cold War between the United States and the Soviet Union.

The house that Lucy and her family lived in had three floors that was free range for her young children. One day, Lucy's son Mark was playing in the third floor attic when he made an amazing discovery. The family was very excited about Mark's find.

Martha Jo said, "On the third floor of our house was an attic; one day when Mark was playing in the attic, he found a suitcase full of old German money. The money was not any good because it was printed before World War II started. The money that was found in our attic was before the country went to Marx as their primary currency. Today, Mark still has a lot of that old German money; he gave a bunch of it away." The picture below shows four samples of the German money which Mark had found in their home in Germany.

During Katie Lucille Walker's time as a soldier's wife in Germany, the world that was experienced by her family was much different and father apart than it is today. As a spouse of a career military husband, there were no regular telephones at their house; cell phones were not even invented; lap top computers were unheard of; and, microwave ovens were a thing in the future. In other words, the world moved at a much slower pace.

During the 1961 and 1962 tour of duty in Germany, communication was primarily by written letters. Letters with a foreign country address took weeks to arrive. It was during this technological state of the world when Lucy was in West Berlin that she received a letter from her mother. The letter was very disturbing to Lucy.

"During the time I was in Germany, I got a letter from my momma. She wrote, 'Your daddy has moved a "one eyed devil" into this house.' I had no idea what mama was talking about. I immediately wrote her back asking what in the world did she mean by saying a 'one eyed devil' because I could not imagine what momma was referring to. I was both amazed and uneasy about what was going on at home in Alabama" recalled Lucy.

Lucy, being somewhat upset, immediately wrote her mother back inquiring about the "one eyed devil." She anxiously waited for a letter from her mother explaining what she was calling a "one eyed devil."

"After a while, I got a letter from my momma telling me that some people call the "one eyed devil" a television. If she could look at that television today, she would know it was truly a one eyed devil," reaffirmed Lucy.

After reading the letter from her mother explaining what the one eyed devil was, Katie Lucille was greatly relieve, but could not stop laughing. She could just imagine her mother and Aunt Cindy thinking the television was so evil that it must be the devil.

Back home in Alabama when Dan Walker turned on the television, Vady's stepmother Cindy Wilbanks Legg, who we called Aunt Cindy, was ready to walk across the pasture back to her small wood frame home. Grandma Vady and Aunt Cindy would not touch the thing; they left the functioning of the "one eyed devil" to Mr. Dan.

If Aunt Cindy was in a conversation with Grandma Vady and Dan turned on the television, she would refuse to watch. Aunt Cindy would even turn her back and get ready to leave the house as soon as possible. Both Aunt Cindy and

Grandma Vady though the television was evil; initially, they would not even watch the television news or other programs.

Cold War Gets Hot

In 1961 in West Berlin, Germany, Lucy and her children found themselves in a hot bed of political unrest. The "Cold War" was raging with the one of the most noted events during this period being the construction of the Berlin Wall. West Berlin was a democracy controlled by the United States and East Berlin was under the communist control of the Soviets.

Asa Lynn, Jo, Mark, and Lucille Walker
Berlin, Germany 1961

Katie Lucille and her family had been in Germany for only four months when Soviet leader Nikita Khrushchev ordered that the border of West Berlin be sealed off and secured by Soviet military forces. In the early hours of Sunday, August 13, 1961, Soviet leader Nikita Khrushchev ordered that the border of West Berlin, Germany, be sealed off and secured by his military forces. He also ordered the construction of a wall to isolate and surround West Berlin begin immediately. People trying to cross the secure border into West Berlin were to be shot on sight. Khrushchev's Cold War push to control Berlin, Germany was in full effect, and Katie Lucille Walker and her children were caught in the middle of the turmoil.

Khrushchev also ordered his troops to kill anyone trying to cross into the United States side of the border. World War II was over, but "Man's inhumanity to man" was not. People trying to cross the secure border from Soviet Communists controlled East Berlin into West Berlin were to be shot on sight. Since Katie Lucille's house was within a few feet of the wall, she and her children witnessed some of the freedom seeking individuals getting killed.

During her time in Germany, Katie Lucille saw the start of construction of the Berlin Wall a few yards from the home where her family was living. From their upstairs window, the family witnessed the Berlin Wall being built. She said, "From our window, we could see them building the wall. The wall was being built about twenty five feet from our house. You could see people trying to jump or cross the wall getting shot dead. I saw a least five people getting killed trying to cross the wall and get into

Berlin Wall Construction

West Berlin. My children and I had to live there for eighteen months while the wall was under construction."

At first it did not seem so bad, but as the construction of the wall continued things began to change. With each passing day, construction crews moved closer and closer to their home. The commotion became more intense. Noise was constant. The roar of engines, the thunder of hammers, the echo of gunfire, and then the screams of death were a daily reminder. Crying, shouting, and firing guns were not uncommon. Everyone knew that sound meant someone had attempted to defect to West Berlin, and another life had ended. Lucy's feelings of uneasiness increased with every thud of a hammer. Lucy was overcome by a sense of urgency; time to go. Desperate, she called her dad.

Martha Jo Walker said, "We lived at number five Berlip Straussa, West Berlin, Germany. All American students went to the American military school at the Tempelhof Air Force Base in West Berlin. I was in the second grade when we got to Germany. While I was in the third grade, Soviet soldiers started forcing all German children ten years old and younger to be taken to East Berlin where they were being brainwashed." The Soviets forces were attempting to take all German children ten years old and under to East Berlin to indoctrinate them in Communism.

According to the account told by Katie Lucille, "There were two little blond haired, blue eyed girls playing in our yard one afternoon. One was my American daughter, and the other was her German friend. A Soviet soldier walked into our yard and snatched the little German Girl. The little American girl was my eight year old daughter Martha Jo Walker." At this point Lucy became fearful of what might happen to her children, and she became a very protective mother.

The following is Martha Jo Walker Wise's account of the story, "My best friend was a German girl who lived next door to our house. She was nine years old. We were both in the third grade. We were playing in our yard just a few feet from our house where Soviet forces were building the Berlin Wall. As we were playing that day close to where the wall was being built, Soviet soldiers come got my friend. They started dragging her toward the East Berlin side of the wall. My friend was screaming and fighting. She finally broke loose from the soldiers and started running toward me."

As Martha Jo was relating the events above, one could sense deep emotional feelings that she was experiencing as she told the story. Tears welled up in her eyes and a tremble came to her lips. It was taking a toll on her emotions to complete the rest of the story.

She said, "I was standing there watching as the Soviet soldiers began shooting at her. She was literally blown apart by the soldiers right in front of me in our yard. It was a brutal and violent scene as I watched her being shot to death. The sight has caused me emotional trouble for most of my life. I will never get over what I witnessed that day. To this day, the image of her being killed in front of me is still very vivid in my mind!"

The Escape

Khrushchev's cold war push to control Berlin, Germany, was in full effect, and Katie Lucille's family was right in the line of fire next to the wall. Since Asa Walker was working in underground security to intercept Soviet intelligence, his life as well as his family was in danger. Katie Lucille Walker and her children were caught in the middle of this Cold War turmoil.

Lucy said, "I knew that Asa along with his other coworkers were issued cyanide capsules to take in case they were captured. There was an emergency, and we did not get to see Asa for several weeks. His captain came by and told me to be prepared if something happened. Knowing that they had given Asa something to end his life in case he was captured was a very scary and difficult time. We were not sure what was going to happen during the time of the crisis."

Shortly after the intense military confrontation between the two superpowers and the building of the wall had started, Katie Lucille Walker called her father Dan Walker. She requested money to pay for her trip back home to Alabama. Dan wired his daughter sufficient funds to get her and the children back home to Alabama. But, United States President John Fitzgerald Kennedy said, "No."

When Lucy tried to make travel arrangements to get her family out of Germany, she was informed that military families were not allowed to leave the country under orders from the President. The United States President John F. Kennedy refused to let any of the military security service families return to their homes in the states during the Berlin crisis.

The Cold War was heating up; people were being threatened and shot on a daily basis. The news media was not allowed to tell the whole story of the danger the secret security service was facing in West Berlin from the Soviet threats. The families of the security service were kept in the dark and not told what was happening during the crisis.

The cement wall separated the city into East Berlin controlled by the Soviet Union and West Berlin controlled by the United States. The barricade was several feet high and topped barbed wire in an attempt to keep the German people controlled by the Communists from going to the free West Berlin. Ultimately more United States military troops were sent to protect the people on the west side of the wall.

Many Germans living in East Berlin tried to escape; few were successful and many were shot and killed. The people in West Berlin began placing wreaths on the wall as a memorial where their friends or relatives had died seeking freedom. Loved ones who had died were memorialized by wreaths that hung on the bloody wall.

Katie Lucille told a story of a Sunday afternoon walk near the wall, "I observed the body of a young man hanging in the barbed wire. He had been trying to cross the barrier, but he was killed when he reached the top of the wall. His lifeless body was left hanging in the wire as a reminder to those who might make an attempt to flee to freedom." Such scenes described by Lucy were not rare occurrences. Ironically, a statue within a few yards of the wall was that of a peace angel.

As the situation became more and more volatile, Lucy grew more concerned for the safety of her children. The military officials were afraid that the situation might get out of hand. They ordered all the security service families to move to a protected location on the base. The military also placed their secret security service men in underground bunkers and did not allow them to return to their families for several weeks.

Martha Jo said, "Everything was going smoothly until they started building that wall. I was going to the military school on base, and daddy was working swing shift. One day daddy went to work and did not return at his usual time. After several days of daddy being gone, momma became very concerned and wanted to know what was going on." But, Katie Lucille got no answers.

Mark, Lynn, Martha Jo, and Asa in Berlin 1961

At the same time, the United States military command in West Berlin ordered the seven or eight families with spouses in the secret service to be moved into one house. Katie Lucille said, "We were moved in with the other wives and children in the building on the base. We were all scared and had no idea what was happening to our husbands. The captain came in and told us to pack one suitcase in case we were going to be overrun. He instructed the wives to dress ourselves and our children like the other Germans, then move into the streets, not let people know we were Americans, and try to blend in with the German civilians."

At the time the families of security personnel were isolated in a secure facility on the base, Lucy was pregnant with her fourth child. During all that disorder, she and her family were moved from their home. Lucy was allowed to bring only one suitcase. They had previously lived in a three story house adjacent to the wall, and they had to leave all the family possessions and furnishing. That was the second time Katie Lucille's family lost all their household belongings.

After several days of isolation with the other families, things begin to happen very fast. The families had no advance warning of a pending move by the military. In the middle of the night, a military transport bus pulled up to the secured facility housing the families. Everyone was ordered to get their things and get on the bus.

Katie Lucille and her children were evacuated from Berlin, Germany, by the United States military. They were not told where or how they were leaving Germany, but they just followed orders. After all the families were loaded on the bus, they were taken to the airport. At Tempelhof Central Airport, the families of the security service personnel were told to board a plane. No one was told were the plane was heading.

Tempelhof Airport where Lucy and her children escaped Germany

Lucy said, "Finally, the military brought a bus and picked up all the families they had isolated for security purposes. They carried us to the airport in the middle of the night and put us on a plane. We had no idea where we were going. All the secret service security families with us left Germany in October 1962; the next day, we landed in England."

At that time, Katie Lucille had not heard from Asa for several days; she did not know if he was dead or alive. She was extremely concerned about his whereabouts, and she was unable to get any information from the military since he was assigned a top secret security clearance. All Lucy could do was hope, wait, and pray for his safe return.

On June 12, 1987, United States President Ronald Reagan attended the 750th anniversary of Berlin, Germany. During his speech at the Brandenburg Gate near the Berlin Wall, President Reagan gave an exhortation to Soviet leader Mikhail Gorbachev to bring down the barrier separating East and West Berlin. President Reagan said, "Mr. Gorbachev, tear down this wall." The actual demolition of the Berlin Wall officially began on June 13, 1990, and was completed in 1992. With the fall of the Berlin Wall and the reunification of Germany, the United States ended a forty nine year American military presence in Germany on January 29, 1993.

Katie Lucille (Lucy) Walker witnessed the Berlin Wall being built, and she lived to see the wall torn down. To her, the wall represented the most vivid image of the Cold War. As she watched on television the Berlin Wall coming down, she experienced a flood of flashbacks of the blood and death at the wall. Horrific images raced through her mind as she recalled those last weeks that she, her children, and other American Security Service families were forced to endure in Germany. Nevertheless, Lucy was relieved to know that finally Berlin would become a city without a barrier separating German families.

Chapter Thirteen

October 1962-Chicksands Air Force Base, London, England

Katie Lucille Walker, her children, and some eight wives and the children of the security personnel left Germany in the middle of the night and landed at the Chicksands Air Force Base, England. After the plane landed, the families were told that they were in England. All the families of security personnel were then transported to their new living quarters.

The move to England was the one exception when the military financed the transfer of Katie Lucille's family from one duty station to another. The night time escape from Germany was the only time that Lucy and her children were moved to another assignment free of charge by the military, and the only time during a move that Lucy did not have to secure money for her travel. All the other moves, the military provided no assistance for the family. Lucy had always made arrangements and had paid all the travel expense for her family to be with Asa Francis Walker, Jr.

When Katie Lucille Walker arrived in England, she was pregnant with her fourth child. She had all the terrible stress of leaving her husband in Berlin, Germany, without knowing what was happening to him. In addition, she had to leave all of her family's possessions in Germany except for the one suitcase that she had been allowed to take to Chicksands Air Force Base in England.

All the security service military families arriving from Berlin were moved into a high rise type apartment building. Their apartment was in a tall stone building with a zigzagged stair case leading to a small, cold room on the third floor. For the next eighteen months, this was to be the home of Katie Lucille and her family.

Katie Lucille lost her baby due to an accident. The following account was given by her daughter Martha Jo Walker Wise. Jo said, "At the time we flew from Germany to England, mother was pregnant, but lost the baby after we got to Chicksands Air Force Base."

Shortly after their arrival in Chicksands, Katie Lucille had an accident. She slipped and fell down those steep zigzagged stairs. Lucy was taken to the base hospital where she remained for a few days. Martha Jo, Mark, and Asa Lynn were left under the care of another family who had been evacuated from West Berlin with Lucy and her children.

Martha Jo said, "When we got off the plane in England, we went into this tall skinny building with zigzagging stairs with several members of each family. Mother was coming up or down the stairs, and her foot slipped and she fell. Mother had to go to the hospital and had a miscarriage. We did not have a baby on the way anymore. All I know is that before she went to the hospital, we were looking forward to having a new baby, but when she came home, there was not going to be a new baby."

As if being far from home with three small children, one suite case of personal belongings, and no household goods was not enough, Lucy had suffered a miscarriage. Now she was alone to deal with the loss of the baby and the unknown fate of her husband. Jo, Mark and Lynn were not aware of their dilemma. They were not old enough to do anything about the situation.

Katie Lucille and her children were saddened by the loss of their expected baby. Asa was not around to comfort his family and knew nothing of the loss of his child until he was finally reunited with his family in England. Asa had not been seen for several days before they left Germany. Lucy had not heard from him for several weeks after they had been moved to England, and the military personnel would not give her any information concerning his whereabouts. Being weak from the miscarriage and sick with worry, Lucy had to rally and prepare to carry on in spite of the outcome.

Lucy was experiencing being alone in a foreign country. Loneliness was an issue faced by military wives especially those living abroad because there were no relatives and few friends. Katie Lucille experienced loneliness because Asa had to be away from his family for a long period of time. Not having an adult family member or friend in the house to talk to and share responsibilities for everyday life was sometimes overwhelming. In addition, being away from home and relatives created a difficult situation when a family member got sick, or as in Lucy's case, fell victim to an accident.

Katie Lucille knew that her husband had been given a cyanide pill to take in case he was captured. For days, she struggled with the idea that the Soviets had been successful in capturing the American Security Service men. For several weeks Lucy had not seen or heard from her husband. Then one day just out of the blue, Asa appeared in England, and the family was reunited. Shortly after Asa's return, Lucy found out that he had gone underground to avoid being captured by the Communists. He was detained there until it was clear that he could be smuggled out of Germany without Soviet detection.

"We found out later that daddy had been put in a secure underground facility in Germany, but while he was gone, we had no money to buy food. We were moved in the middle of the night with one suitcase. We had nothing but the clothes in our suitcase," recalled Martha Jo. Since Asa received his pay only once a month and he was not around to collect his money, Lucy had to live on what little money she had in her possession. For several weeks, Katie Lucille and her children struggled to find a way to get enough food to eat and survive during the time that Asa was kept underground by his commanding officers.

Martha Jo said, "About five weeks after we had arrived in England, my daddy just showed up at the door. He had been in an underground facility in West Berlin, Germany. Because he was in the security service and was in danger of being killed or kidnapped by the Soviet spies, we were not told anything about his whereabouts. Of course, the news of the loss of our baby was a sad thing to tell our daddy about."

Katie Lucille Walker was a strong woman in many ways. She had been raised by a father who showed great strength physically and emotionally, but at the same time her father was a very positive man of high Christian beliefs. Lucy had inherited all those characteristics. She weathered the storms of life with an attitude of strength and a positive outlook in the most distressful and dreadful situations. To her, life must go on in a productive way because that was just the way she was raised. The loss of her baby and the near loss of her husband were things she took in stride. Again, she proved to be a very strong southern woman who would continue her confident role as a mother and soldier's wife.

From the fall of 1962 until he returned to the United States in the spring of 1964, Asa F. Walker worked with the security service at Chicksands Air Force

Base. The base was originally bought by the British Crown of Commissioners on April 15, 1936, to be used by the Royal Navy. After some nine months, the Royal Air Force took over the operations for signal intelligence collection. During World War II, the base was important in intercepting and collecting German communications.

Chicksands was subleased to the United States Air Force in 1950. In the fall of 1962, Asa Francis Walker, Jr. served on the base with the radio squadron which was responsible for continued communications and signal intelligence collection during the Cold War. The Royal Air Force acted as the host for the United States Air Force units including the United States Air Force Security Squadron in which Asa served. Later, the security squadron became the Electronic Security Group.

In England, Asa continued to monitor military intelligence activities during the Cold War. Shortly after the installation of a radar antenna array of 1,443 feet in diameter that formed a part of the "Iron Horse" network, Asa continued to gather security information. Incidentally, this was part of the same "Iron Horse" radar system on which Asa had collected intelligence while serving in Alaska.

Th particular antenna array at Chicksands was called the "Elephant Cage." The radar system was dismantled in 1996 when the United States Air Force withdrew from Chicksands and turned the area back over to the British. At Chicksands, Asa had just over a year left in his assignment when his family escaped the turmoil in West Berlin, so they spent the remainder of that tour of duty in England.

Katie Lucille said, "In England, we spent eighteen months of a three year tour that was supposed to be spent in Germany. While in England, we lived on base which was just outside the City of London. Even though the base was next to the city, we would roam over the big green fields and let the kids fly kites." The weather in London was often cloudy, cold and damp, but the children still found time to play outside without worry of being taken by Soviet soldiers. They would ride their bicycles along the hedge rows and across the green fields of the English countryside.

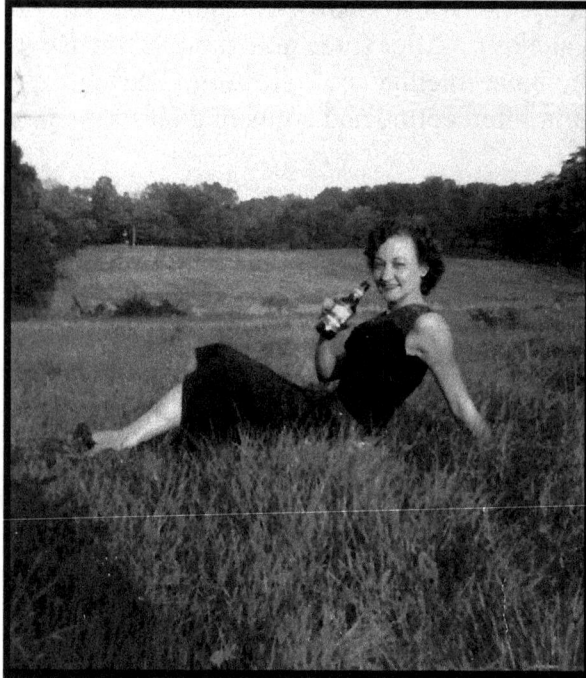

Lucy enjoying the green grass

According to Lucy, "The time in England was more like the United States and was not as intense as it had been in Germany."

After Asa was reunited with his family, Lucy regained her strength and the family moved to new quarters. Life returned to normal if there was any such thing. Martha Jo and Mark attended the base school and spent their free time playing with their little brother Asa Lynn.

Martha Jo said, "I think I was in the fourth grade when we got to England. I went to the military school on base. Every military school used the same curriculum and same book in all their grades and classes. Therefore, when we moved, I did not get behind because the teachers taught the same courses the same way that I had been taught before moving."

Death of President John F. Kennedy

Most people born in the 1940's and 1950's can remember where they were and what they were doing on November 22, 1963. The people of the United States seemed to be in a state mourning because their beloved President John F. Kennedy had been shot, but that was not the case for all Americans.

According to Martha Jo, those Americans who had experienced the relocation from West Berlin, Germany, to Chicksands did not share in the grief. Lucy's family had been at Chicksands Air Force Base in England for a little over a year when United States President John F. Kennedy was assassinated on November 22, 1963.

Remembering the death of President Kennedy, Katie Lucille said, "There was a big party on the base, especially all of us that escaped from Germany and were refused permission to come back to the states by Kennedy." It seemed that the majority of the military personnel were glad that Kennedy was no long President of the United States and Commander in Chief of the armed forces.

Martha Jo Walker Wise said, "The reason that the families were refused permission to leave Berlin was because they were in a military family. It appeared that most at the base were proud that John F. Kennedy was no longer president of the United States."

Back home in Alabama, most people mourned the death of their young president who was a World War II hero. That sentiment was not shared by all, especially those families associated with the secret service who were originally not allowed to leave Berlin, Germany, by then President John F. Kennedy.

Martha Jo said, "There was celebrating in the streets, people were getting drunk, and they were rejoicing because of the death of President Kennedy. As a child of nine years old, it appeared that all the military personnel on the base were happy that Kennedy was assassinated."

Beatle Mania

Not long after the death of President Kennedy, Katie Lucille found out that The Beatles were performing near their home. She took Jo to see them in concert. They had not reached the peak of fame that they would later achieve, but Lucy and Martha Jo would get a chance to see them perform their music. Lucy said, "While we were in England, we got to see The Beatles before they became famous."

Katie Lucille remembered the young British group of musicians who had descended on London and were gaining a very favorable reputation. The new and upcoming band was playing in the park near their home. She thought that Martha Jo would enjoy the music so Lucy took her to the concert.

Little did Lucy and Jo realize that they were watching music history unfold. That history making band would capture the hearts of music lovers around the world. However, in 1963, Lucy and Jo watched young girls jump to their feet and start screaming when The Beatles-John Lennon, Paul McCartney, George Harrison, and Ringo Starr-came on stage. They sang three of their hits; *"I Saw Her Standing There," "I Want to Hold Your Hand,"and"All My Loving."*

Martha Jo was really excited to see the group perform." She said, "I was like nine or ten years old, and we went to a concert in a park in London where The Beatles were performing. It was just a group of four guys playing music. It did not dawn on us until later when we realized who we actually saw."

The Beatles had not yet made their debut in the United States, but their popularity was growing everywhere. It would not be until Sunday night on February 9, 1964, that The Beatles would appear on the Ed Sullivan Show on American television for the first time. That night, approximately seventy three million American fans watched their performance. Martha Jo said, "Later, I got to see The Beatles on television when we got back to the states!"

In August 1964, The Beatles kicked off their first musical tour in the United States. During their first concert in San Francisco, they sang *"A Hard Day's Night," "I Want to Hold Your Hand,"*and*"Eight Days a Week"* as well as many other songs that they would later record.

In January 1969, The Beatles performed live for the last time as a group. Their last performance was on the roof of the headquarters of Apple Records in London, England. After ten years of working together, The Beatles went their separate ways. Beatle mania was declining.

Chapter Fourteen

April 1964-Fort George G. Meade, Maryland, USA

In early 1964, Asa Walker got orders to report to Fort George G. Mead in Maryland. The family had already spent one tour of duty in Maryland, and they were excited to return for another three year period on familiar ground in the United States.

By April, Asa and Lucy were again at Fort Mead, Maryland, for the second time. During this assignment, Asa and Lucy bought a house in Silver Spring, Maryland. The City of Silver Spring was named from the mica flakes that mixed with the water flowing from a spring. The spring was first discovered and named by Francis Preston Blair along with his daughter Elizabeth in 1840 after they observed the spring sparkling like silver because of the mica chips.

Two years after discovery of the spring, Francis Preston Blair completed a twenty-room mansion nearby that he called Silver Spring; the spacious home stood until 1954. Blair's son Montgomery became Postmaster General for Abraham Lincoln; Lincoln visited the Silver Spring mansion many times. Acorn Park is believed to be the site of the original spring. The major business district of Silver Spring lies at the north corner of Washington, D.C.

Asa Walker's sister Nora lived in Washington, D.C., during his two tours of military duty. She had moved from Hartselle, Alabama, to live with Asa and Lucy shortly after they were married during their first tour at Fort Meade. During Asa and Lucy's the second duty assignment at Fort George G. Meade, the house they bought at Silver Spring was near Nora, and they moved Asa's mother into their home.

"Nora stayed in Washington, D.C. in that same apartment as long as she was there. She finally got on at Belks department store and saved over two hundred thousand dollars in twenty five dollar savings bonds. After Asa retired and we moved close to my old home at Danville, Nora moved back to Alabama," said Lucy.

Martha Jo Walker Wise said, "Later in life, Nora went into the present-day Country Cottage nursing home in Falkville, Alabama. Five days out of seven, I was with Nora for her last twelve years. I did that without any pay. Her money was used to pay for her assisted living. Her alimony was $450.00 per month. The money came from shares in Sunoco Oil. Nora died in 2012."

Asa's mother Letha Walker had moved from Alabama to Maryland to live with Lucy and Asa. Letha was suffering from dementia, and she was sick most of the time she lived with the family. Jo said, "Daddy's mother Letha came to live with us. She was sick all the time, and she would not let any doctor see her except Doctor Hardy. It made no difference where we carried her, she always saw Doctor Hardy who was the doctor on the soap opera General Hospital. Every day between three thirty and four o'clock, we had to be quite so she could watch General Hospital. Letha was also Nora's mom, and we lived in the same community."

Jo said, "Before we left England coming back to the United States, mother was pregnant with another baby. Shortly after we arrive in Silver Spring, Maryland, mother lost her second baby. My mother was under a lot of stress during the second tour in Maryland. Daddy's mother moved in with us, and it made the situation more difficult and put a strain on our family life."

The stress that Lucy was dealing with probably contributed to her losing the baby. Lucy was contending with the sickness cause by the pregnancy. In addition on a daily basis, she had to deal with Asa's mother who was suffering from dementia. Living with her senile mother-in-law was very stressful to Katie Lucille during her pregnancy. After Lucy's second miscarriage, she and Asa decided not to have additional children.

Once again, Lucy bounced back from the loss of another baby, and she continued her life as usual. She would invite the base commanders to their house for dinner. The children would be dressed in the finest clothes that she had made.

According to Martha Jo, "When we were having the important people for dinner, mama would put us all in the same outfits; one was always white with contrasting trim. The boys wore one piece rompers with navy trim, and I wore a white dress with navy trim. We were threatened not to make a move or mess-up our clothes before the company got there."

Not only were the children dressed in their best, so was the dining table. In true southern tradition, a white, starched and ironed linen table cloth was draped over the table and matching white linen napkins were properly placed. No matter where they were stationed, the fine crystal was unpacked. Lucy decorated her house and got out her best china, and she cooked her favorite southern foods which were always delicious

Martha Jo said, "Mother would dress us up in white clothes that she had made and invite the base commanders to our house. She made us be quite and mind our manners. If we did not mind, mother would spank us with her shoe. One time, my daddy whipped me three times before he finally stopped. After the third spanking, I kept my mouth shut. Mother wanted us to be number one. She wanted my dad to get the highest rake possible and make more money."

Asa would not necessarily go along with all the pomp and ceremony. According to Jo, "He would sometimes come out in his shorts and Hawaii style shirt." It made no difference to Lucy how Asa dressed. She was going to do everything in her power to promote and support her husband. That is just the way she lived life as a soldier's wife.

According to Martha Jo, "About two years after mother lost the baby when we first got to Maryland, she gave birth to my baby sister. Cynthia was considered our miracle baby. She was an 'oops' and was not planned for according to my mother. Cynthia was born on January 2, 1966, at the hospital at Fort George G. Meade. After Cynthia was born, momma and daddy decided since there was such an age difference that they might as well have another baby for Cynthia to grow up with."

Family Reunion

About seven months after the birth of Cynthia, Asa's family was planning to come home to Alabama on leave from Fort George G. Mead, Maryland. This furlough was in July 1966. Since Katie Lucille, Asa, and their children would not be home long enough to visit all her brothers and sisters, the furlough provided an opportunity for everyone to get together for the family reunion. Since Lucy's family would be in Alabama for a short stay, the Walker parents and siblings planned a reunion for her family at Brushy Lake in William B. Bankhead National Forest.

The family reunion was planned well in advance of the arrival of Katie Lucille, Asa, and their children. Dan Walker's family spread the word about the reunion. Letters telling the time, date, and place of the picnic were sent to family members. Since no one in the Walker family had telephones, the letters were mailed several days in advance in order to inform all Lucy's siblings and kinfolks of the big event. It was expected that all of Lucy's brothers and sisters along with most nieces and nephews attended the big gathering at Brushy Lake in the forest.

Last Dan Walker Family gathering at Brushy Lake

Big family reunions were usually every three years since this would coincide with Asa's furlough. Sometimes family members would meet at Dan and Vady Walker's home for a big Sunday lunch, and on other occasions, it was at a different location. For one reason or another, some family members were always missing, but at Brushy Lake, the parents and all the siblings were present for the big event.

With a large extended family, it was rare that everyone could get together. Travel was not as easy then as it is today, and like Lucy, some family members had moved away from Alabama. Some folks had traveled great distances to get there, so they were not expected to bring food.

Food was always a very important component of a Walker reunion. People always talked about Vady Walker's huge biscuits or maybe it was Aunt Lodean's delicious coconut cake. Of course, the menu always included southern fried chicken which was cooked in hog lard that gave the meat its unique flavor. All sorts of fresh garden vegetables including fried okra, fried squash, and fried potatoes that were also cooked in hog lard were on the picnic table. Big slices of red tomatoes were fresh from the garden. Children were running around with corn on the cob in their hands. Platters of fried apple and peach pies as well as home ice cream were served for desserts. Members of the Walker family consumed gallons of ice cold sweet tea and lemonade.

Reunions stirred childhood memories in Katie Lucille and her siblings. They talked about growing up and being together as one big family. Lucy was introduced to new babies and new spouses of nieces and nephews. She loved greeting old family members and new in-laws of each of her siblings with hugs, kisses, and handshakes. With a big smile on her face, Katie Lucille always greeted her family members with true compassion. One could feel the love she had for her family.

I will never forget my Aunt Lucille making me and my males cousins feel so great. She would always say, "Those Walker men are just very handsome." She was the only aunt that would tell us how handsome we were. Her statement always brought a smile to my face. She had no idea how great that made me feel, but maybe she did and that was her way of lifting my spirits. Such was the character and compassion of my precious and wonderful aunt. I then understood why my dad Brady Walker was so close to his baby sister Katie Lucille Walker.

Martha Jo Walker Wise said, "I was only in Alabama four times before my high school graduation and this was one of those times. We had returned to the states two years earlier from England and were living at Silver Spring, Maryland, where Cynthia was born on January 2, 1966. At the time of the reunion at Brushy Lake, I was twelve years old."

The most memorable Walker family reunion that comes to mind was the one held at Brushy Lake in Lawrence County, Alabama, in July 1966. It was the last reunion that both Dan and Vady would attend. All the Walker family was so thankful to have snapshots of the memorable occasion. Taking pictures ranked right up there with talking and eating. Some kinfolks showed off their new cars while others showed off their new babies.

One of the new babies belonged to my sister Diane Walker Thrasher. She had a baby boy who she named Ocie Bradly (Brad) Thrasher. Brad was born on December 10, 1965. At the Walker reunion, a picture was taken of Brad and Cynthia. Brad was about eight months old and Cynthia, daughter of Katie Lucille Walker, was seven months old.

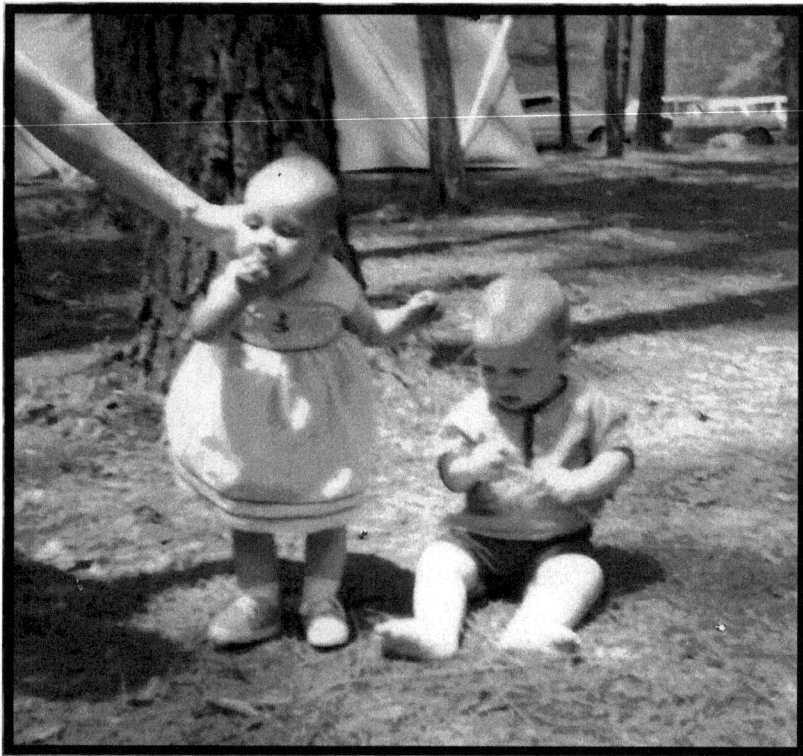

Cynthia Walker and Brad Thrasher at Brushy Creek
July 1966 Walker Family Reunion

Cynthia and Brad were about the same age and had just started standing and trying to walk. In the picture below are Cynthia and her cousin Brad.

Cynthia, who was attempting to stand, was being supported by Lucy to keep her from falling.

After Lucy's family returned to Asa's military duty station, her parents and siblings usually did not see or hear from her again except by letters or until the next reunion or change in military assignments. Each time the family got to be with Lucy and her kids, they celebrated the life of their extended family and renewed their bonds.

Orders for Italy

Once Katie Lucille's family got back to Maryland in the summer of 1966, she began preparing for another move that she knew was coming within seven months. In the spring of 1967 after being at Silver Spring, Maryland, for three years, Asa got orders to report to San Vito Air Force Base at Brindisi, Italy.

Asa's tour of duty at Fort Meade had been the longest the military family had lived in one place, but they were ready for the move to Italy. The great adventure of Asa and Lucy was not complete. Lucy's dream of seeing the world was not finished; therefore, with much anxious excitement, she began preparing her growing family for another move.

Most of the time, Katie Lucille was uprooting her children every eighteen months or less so that they could be near their father. While Asa was in the military, moving on a regular basis was a way of life, and something that Lucy accepted as a soldier's wife. She said, "Moving was not a big deal. It was something that I knew was going to happen often, and I was ready on a moment's notice."

After the military sent Asa to Italy, Katie Lucille packed up her things as usual and headed to her parents' home at Danville for a short stay. During this time, Lucy was several months pregnant. As an expectant mother, she had to make all the arrangements for her and her four kids to fly to Italy to be with her husband.

With tears, kisses, and hugs, she bid farewell to her mother and daddy who she knew that she would not see until the assignment in Italy was over. Little did Katie Lucille know that when she left home this time that it would be the last time that she would see her beloved mother. Lucy would only get to visit her mother's burial site, and she would place flowers upon her mother's grave.

Katie Lucille visited her parents as often as possible, and sad farewells were a part of her life. Saying goodbye to her mom and dad never got easy for Katie Lucille. As I was conducting interviews with Aunt Lucille for this book, I could hear the sadness in her voice when she talked about leaving her parents. At the same time, I could sense the joy she felt by being with her husband and by keeping her own family together during the difficult times as a soldier's wife.

Chapter Fifteen

March 1967-San Vito Air Force Base, Brindisi, Italy

Katie Lucille was seven months pregnant when she left her Alabama home for Italy. Unknowingly, she had said a last goodbye to her mother; her father would live for another goodbye. Lucy and her four children were heading to Brindisi, Italy, to be with Asa Francis Walker, Jr. With her four children in tow and another one on the way, Katie Lucille was going to a foreign country not knowing what she would be facing when she got there.

Asa was working at the United States Air Force base located between Brindisi and San Vito dei Normanni, Italy. The base was seven miles north to northwest of Brindisi, Apulia, between the Port of Brindisi on the Adriatic Sea and the town of San Vito dei Normanni, Italy. The San Vito base was too small for a runway and flight line, so fixed-wing aircraft operated from the nearby Italian Air Force Base.

The small base to which Asa was assigned was only three hundred and eighteen acres. Since the San Vito base was about three hundred miles southeast of Rome on Italy's boot heel, most of the military personnel and their families flew from the United States to the major airport in Rome. From Rome, they would travel to the San Vito base.

Lucy's family lived off base on the shores of the beautiful Adriatic Sea in a well preserved historic sea side home. The family lived in the Italian village of Speciola which was a fishing community located on the sea coast. The town had cobblestone streets which were still being used when Asa and Katie Lucille's family arrived.

AL COMANDO STAZIONE CARABINIERI DI CAROVIGNO (BR.)

Il sottoscritto, WALKER Asa, nato a Hartselle, Alabama,

USA, il 28 Aprile 1928, Sorg. Magg. USAF in servizio presso

il 6917th Security Group, USAFSS, San Vito dei Normanni Air

Station, residente a Specchiolla, Villa Dei Pini, dichiara il

possesso delle sottoindicate armi da fuoco:

1. Un fucile "Iver Johnson", cal. 12, matricola No.85102

2. Un fucile "H & R", cal. 12, matricola No. N/N

3. Una carabina "Stevens", mod. 65, cal.22, matricola No.N/N

4. Una pistola "Mary Arms", cal. 22, matricola 301232.

All'uopo dichiara di aver acquistato le armi suddette

negli Stati Uniti d'America.

In fede.

Specchiolla, 15 Maggio 1967

ASA WALKER
TSGT, USAF

Si attesta che il dichiarante presta servizio presso

questa Base USAFSS.

STAZIONE DI CAROVIGNO

VISTO: si conferma l'avvenuta denunzia e la legit-
tima provenienza dell'Arma. la stessa è registrata
al n.1 della lettera W della rubrica delle Armi di
di questo Comando.
Carm   IL MARESCIALLO MAGGIORE

Aunt Lucille said, "While in Italy, we lived in a beautiful villa in the heel of the boot of Italy. The house was on the shores of the Adriatic Sea. The home had marble floors, marble pillars, and it was next to other gorgeous houses along the sea coast."

Lucy's new Italian home was a lavish villa for that time and place. It was located on the southern coast of Italy overlooking the Adriatic Sea. The multilevel villa towered above the cobblestone street that hugged the water's edge.

Lucy said, "The Adriatic Sea was beautiful but nasty and smelled bad." The sea was only a short distance from the front door of their home. The scene was beautiful, but area had a smell like that of sewage. The water was polluted, and the sea was unfit to enter.

"From our home, we would watch the local fishermen bring in lots of fish. Fishermen cleaned their fish and threw the remains in the water. The fishermen would catch fish and pinch their heads off and eat them raw. However, the local people ate those fish and did not seem to have a problem. I would not let my family eat those fish because the sewage ran right into the sea," stated Katie Lucille.

Lucy would not allow her children to eat the fish from the sea, nor would she not allow them to drink the tap water in their home. The house where her family lived did not have a water filter. She said, "The public water was so bad that we got water from the base or from a neighbor who had a water filter."

The village was surrounded by artichoke fields and grape vineyards. While living nearby, Lucy toured a grape vineyard and winery where the local people were making that great Italian wine. She told the story of women bringing bunches of grapes from the vineyards to the winery in their aprons or baskets. They dumped the grapes into a large round vat of some sort. Then the women took their shoes off, and, without washing their dirty feet, climbed into the vat and stomped the grapes to mash the juice out. The juice was then poured into containers and allowed to ferment into wine. Although she was familiar with different cultural practices, Lucy found it a little strange that the people did not seem at all concerned with their lack of hygiene.

The hillsides around the village of Speciola were utilized by shepherds who watched over their flocks of hundreds of sheep. Most of the sheep herders were poor subsistence farmers that depended on their flocks of sheep for survival. They lived off the land and whatever they could do to survive even at the expense of others.

"Our home did not have glass in the windows, but it had louvers and screens in the windows because most of the time the weather was very warm," according to Lucy. Occasionally, when heat was need for keeping the house warm, heating oil was used, and oil was also used for cooking. Asa kept large barrels of kerosene that was used for heating and cooking stored outside the home.

Lucy said, "One day when we were at home, two sheep herders came to our house and loaded a barrel of our oil on their truck. I had a pistol that I held up to the window. Jo and I were there and they could see us, but it did not stop them from just going ahead and stealing the oil that we used for cooking and heating." Apparently, those sheep herders felt entitled to use anything they could find that they needed for their survival. There was nothing that Lucy could do, so Asa just bought more oil.

That was not the only problem the family had with their heating oil or kerosene. Martha Jo said, "One day when Cynthia was just a toddler, she got some of the kerosene that I had left on the window frame in a small bottle. I had started doing oil on canvas painting and used the kerosene as paint thinner. Cynthia had several big drinks of the kerosene before we realized what she had done. This created an emergency medical situation and great concern. Cynthia was carried to the nearest medical facility. She developed chemically induced pneumonia, but she survived and had no bad after affects."

Asa worked swing shift at San Vito which opened in 1960, some seven years before he arrived. The base was staffed with support personnel and equipment of the 6900th Security Wing. It became a primary installation of the United States Air Force Security Service on March 1, 1961. In 1964, a high frequency monitoring and receiving system of a large circular antenna array known as the "Iron Horse" which assisted in worldwide coverage was installed at San Vito.

Asa would again work with this massive radar system which was operated by the United States Air Force. He had previously worked with the "Iron Horse" system in Alaska and Chicksands, England. During the time he spent at San Vito Air Force Base, Asa Francis Walker, Jr. was gathering and interpreting vital military information with the security service. He worked at the facility which hosted United States military intelligence personnel for some thirty four years.

During the Cold War, the primary purpose of the San Vito base was to intercept and analyze electronic transmissions of enemy nations. The base closed in October 1994 as part of the United States military drawdown. In December 2001, the United States Air Force contracted the removal of the "Iron Horse" antennae array at the San Vito Air Force Base. In 2003, the United States turned the base back over to the Italian government.

Even though Asa spent a great deal of time at work, he also had time to get his boys involved in baseball with the other military lads. The American military families had their own base league where their children could participate in a traditional United States sport. Asa's oldest son Mark played shortstop, and

Asa Lynn played as second baseman. The boys participated in base league baseball while Asa was serving in the military, and it was primarily Lucy's job to get her boys to baseball practice and to their games.

On one particular day, Katie Lucille was taking her young sons to the baseball practice in the family's big Oldsmobile car. A man and woman were walking their dog along the road. As Lucy approached the couple, their dog ran right in front of the car. The little dog was no match for the big car. The little dog ran under the wheels of the car; the accident was unavoidable.

Lucy did not try to dodge the dog, because she knew if she had she would have hit the man and woman. Unable to stop, she ran over the animal and kept going. Needless to say, her children were devastated.

Asa Lynn asked his mother, "Why did you not try to miss that dog?"

His mother related the following story. "When I was at home on the farm in Alabama, a man was coming down the road in front of our house at a pretty high speed for that day. Some of our chickens were in the old road and the man swerved to miss the chickens. He hit the big oak tree in our front yard and killed himself along with several of the chickens. I was not about to take a chance of us having a wreck."

Lucy was not insensitive to pets, but she was protective of her children. And, she would do anything in her power to keep her children safe.

Wheelus Air Force Base, Tripoli, Libya

Katie Lucille was pregnant with her last child Roger when she arrived in Italy. There was not a hospital nearby in Italy that was equipped to deliver the baby. In order to have her baby in a hospital, Lucy had to fly across the Mediterranean Sea to United States controlled Wheelus Air Force Base in Tripoli, Libya.

In most all military assignments of Uncle Ace, Aunt Lucille was left to get to her husband with her children the best way she could arrange. This trip was no different. As it was most of the time, Katie Lucille had to travel to Libya by herself. On this occasion, she had to fly to Tripoli less than a month before the baby was to be born because of the danger of flying when she was close to her delivery date. Unaware of the political unrest, Lucy boarded a plane and headed to Tripoli. Soon, she would be facing the greatest danger of her lifetime.

At the time of Katie Lucille's arrival in Tripoli, King Idris I was the ruler of Libya. During Idris reign of power, political unrest was heightened by one of his military officers by the name of Colonel Muammar Muhammad Abu Minyar al-Gaddafi. The conflict turned into a military revolt to control Libya. Some two years later in September 1969, Colonel Gaddafi was successful in the overthrow of King Idris I, and he took control of Libya as its dictator. Before the revolution, the United States and Libya had reached an agreement over the withdrawal from Wheelus Air Force Base. But, the base was not officially turned over to the new Libyan government controlled by Colonel Gaddafi until June 11, 1970.

"While we were in Italy, I was pregnant with Roger. Since there was no hospital nearby, I was sent to Tripoli, Libya, three weeks before I was supposed to deliver. Roger was born in Tripoli, Libya, on June 6, 1967, at the time of the Libyan military revolt and war broke out," recalled Lucy.

Gaddafi's revolution got started during the time Lucy was in Libya to have her baby. The United States airbase in Tripoli, Libya, was falling into the hands of Dictator Muammar Gaddafi. Lucy said, "I was in Libya to witness the start of the war that put Gaddafi into power."

When Lucy got off the plane in Libya, she went to the base hospital where she met a young American black girl who was there to have her first baby. Katie Lucille found out that the young girl was also a soldier's wife who was stationed at the same base in San Vito, Italy. When Lucy and the young American girl from the base in Italy were in the Wheelus Air Force Base hospital they were taken care of by a Muslim doctor and Muslim nurses. Lucy said, "The nurses only had one eye visible and were totally covered."

Katie Lucille Walker was unaware that within a short time she would be facing a life threatening situation. During her hospital stay, Muammar Gaddafi was starting his attacks on the United States controlled Wheelus Air Force Base in Tripoli. She said, "The attackers cut off the water supply and the electricity to the hospital."

The revolt in Libya got very intense the day that Katie Lucille Walker was induced to give birth to her fifth child Roger. "The doctor put both the young girl and me into labor. With the assistance of Muslim nurses, he delivered our babies." Roger Walker was born to Lucy and Asa under those adverse conditions.

Lucy said, "After our babies were delivered, the Muslim doctor and nurses told us that we were on our own and left us in the hospital by ourselves." Katie Lucille realized their danger when she saw the hospital staff hurriedly leaving. She knew that they would have to find their own way to safety. With the empty hospital and the sounds of war everywhere, Lucy was convinced that their only hope of survival was to find a United States aircraft to get them out of the country. In that dire situation, she told the young black girl, "We got to get out of here and fast."

Katie Lucille realized that the situation they were in was very dangerous. Even though she and the young girl had been induced and had just delivered their babies, she knew that they could not wait for help. Lucy had no idea that anyone was aware of their presence since sights and sounds of war were happening all around the hospital where they were.

Lucy said, "I told the young girl that we better get out of this hospital and find an airplane out of this country." During the night, the two women grabbed wheel chairs and diapers then made their way out of that dark hospital and into the streets filled with the chaos of war. It was in these dire straits that the two women and their newborn babies wheeled themselves toward the airfield.

"The black girl and I found two wheel chairs. We forgot about trying to find our suitcases. Since we were dressed only in hospital gowns, we grabbed a bunch of baby diapers to cover our bodies and our babies. We had just given birth to our babies, and our gowns were wet from breast milk and the birthing process. We unfolded some of the diapers and used them to cover our bodies and our babies. Even though we had just delivered our babies, we made a mad rush for the airfield in those wheel chairs," Lucy recalled.

The thing that might have saved their lives or might have cost them their lives was that they were American women who had newborn babies. The two mothers and their new babies did not have clothes to wear, but that was not a problem at the time. Getting their babies to safety was the most compelling factor in the mist the turmoil that was occurring around the hospital.

Clutching their babies to their breasts, Katie Lucille and the other mother rolled their wheelchairs down the dark hospital halls to the nearest exit they could find. They frantically fled into chaotic conditions on the street in front of the hospital. In the terror of the night, lights were flashing in the dark streets. People were running for their lives. Gun shots could be heard all around the area. Vicious dogs were barking and growling nearby. Lucy's heart pounded. She knew that they had to get to the airstrip, and she prayed there would be a plane that could get them and their babies to safety.

She was uncertain as to whether or not they could get out of the country alive. Things had deteriorated so fast that all the hospital staff had abandoned the facility and fled for their lives. The hospital had lost all power and water. The hospital and air force base was under a heavy attack by Colonel Gaddafi's military forces.

Lucy said, "Gaddafi's troops were surrounding the air base and had big vicious dogs. Gunshots were going on all around the area. I could see and hear all of those mean looking dogs that were everywhere growling and barking. The sounds of dogs, gunshots, and explosives were extremely terrifying. The sounds of war were all around us, but I knew we had to find a way to get out of the country."

The echo of gunfire and the sound of barking dogs seemed to be getting closer and closer by the second. Lucy said, "I was more afraid of the dogs than I was of getting shot." Knowing that the dogs would be able to pick up the scent of the new born babies that they carried in their arms, Lucy and her companion were spurred on by a desire for the survival for their infants.

Katie Lucille took the lead and propelled her wheel chair as fast as she possibly could and urged her companion to keep up. Deep down, she knew their only chance of survival was keeping ahead of the dogs. The horrifying sounds of the night were closing in, but they were almost to the airfield. Lucy knew that they had a chance of living through the chaos if they could just hold on for a few more minutes. She prayed as she fought to hold back her tears. She knew that Asa and her children were waiting for her return home. Despite being caught in the middle of a war zone, she intended to make it home safely with her newborn baby boy.

Katie Lucille said, "At the first plane we came to, they had a ramp that was being used to load wounded soldiers and other American patients." Lucy confronted the pilot, "We are Americans and we got to get out of this country; our husbands are at the San Vito Air Force Base in Bridisi, Italy."

"This plane is going to Athens, Greece," replied the pilot.

"I do not care where you are going as long as we can get out of this country before we get killed. Even though we did not have any identification and were dressed in hospital gowns covered with baby diapers, the pilot allowed us and our babies to board the plane," Katie Lucille said.

The two women had given birth a few hours earlier. They were clothed only in the hospital gowns that they wore when they delivered their babies. They were in wheel chairs and partially covered with baby diapers, but they were American citizens and that was an American plane. Lucy was determined to board that plane out of the country. The pilot recognized the desperate situation the women were in and allowed them on the plane. Katie Lucille's determination saved four lives that day.

"The black girl and her baby and I and my baby boarded the plane that was filled with wounded soldiers and one casualty. As we were flying across the Mediterranean Sea, a soldier next to me died," sadly confided Katie Lucille. She knew in her heart that the death of the soldier she just witnessed could have been her and her new baby son. Her heart sank and again she fought to hold back the tears, but as always she knew she had to be strong.

"After we landed in Athens, Greece, a lady at the terminal with the airport security asked me for identification. I told her to just look at me! I was lucky to get out of that country alive with my baby. The black girl and I waited together at the airport in Athens, Greece, until they got us a flight back to Italy," stated Lucy.

After a few days of traveling from Tripoli, Libya, to Athens, Greece, they were flown to Rome, Italy. From there, they traveled back to the San Vito base.

Katie Lucille Walker was exhausted but much relieved and elated to be reunited with her family at home in Speciola, Italy.

Thankfully, Katie Lucille somehow had survived the horrifying ordeal. After being reunited with Asa and her children, she realized that she did not know the name of the young black girl with whom she had endured those life threatening hours in Tripoli, Libya. Lucy would never forget that frightened young mother and their painful experience from the jaws of death.

The frightening experience in Libya was burned into her memory as one of the most dangerous situations that she recalled ever being involved during her time as a soldier's wife. The events were the most dangerous that Katie Lucille Walker faced in all the years of following her husband all over the world to various military bases.

Shortly after Katie Lucille's escape from Tripoli, the United States military destroyed most of Wheelus Air Force Base before it fell into the hands of Colonel Gaddafi. A retired military officer told of seeing the buildings and facilities destroyed by explosives just before he left the base.

Years later after she had returned to her home in Alabama, Katie Lucille would relive her terrifying experience in Tripoli, Libya, as she watched the news cast of Colonel Gaddafi being overthrown by his own people. According to the news report, Colonel Muammar Muhammad Abu Minyar al-Gaddafi was born about 1942, and he died during a revolution of his people on October 20, 2011. He ruled Libya for some forty two years before he was overthrown during the Libyan revolution that was sparked by other countries in the area successfully removing their dictator leaders. Katie Lucille Walker said, "I witnessed Gaddafi coming into power, and I also lived to see him overthrown by his own people."

The family picture on the next page was taken just five weeks after Katie Lucille's terrifying experience in Libya. She had returned to her home in Speciola, Italy, where the family's military portrait was taken.

Asa, Lucy, Jo, Lynn, Roger (5 weeks), Mark, and Cynthia

Back Home in Alabama

Back home in Morgan County, Alabama, on September 9, 1967, Dan Walker had decided it was a perfect morning for a little fishing trip. He knew he needed fish bait, and fiddle worms would be just the thing to catch some fish. During breakfast, Dan told Vady that he was going to walk up the hill to the woods behind their house and try to fiddle some worms.

Vady replied that she had heard of fiddling worms all of her life, but she had never actually seen anyone fiddle worms. Dan asked if she would like to go along; of course, she was anxious to walk with him. Vady was wearing her flour sack print apron, her sun bonnet, and her ole lady comfort shoes; so she was ready to go.

Fiddling worms did not require many tools. All Dan needed was a small bucket and a handsaw. With tools in hand, Dan led the way across the back yard, up the narrow farm road, passed the garden, and up a little grade towards the terraced field where the cotton had been harvested. The field was one terrace after the other to keep the rows from washing away during heavy rains.

The crest of the hill was about a quarter of a mile from the house. As Dan and Vady approached the tree line, the terrain grew steeper. Vady was beginning to get a bit winded and had to take a short rest. After catching her breath and a few minutes to rest, she was up and ready to complete their adventure and watch how worms were fiddled to the top of the ground.

Near the edge of the tree line, they pick their way through a dense area of weeds and bushes. Dan and Vady continue a short distance into the woods. Dan slowed his pace and began looking at each little bush. After checking several small saplings, he settled on one that he thought would be productive. He sawed the little tree off about a foot above the ground and began sawing across the trunk while Vady watched. Sure enough, sawing the sapling sent vibrations along the roots into the ground. Very soon, the fiddling process brought the huge, long, slimy worms crawling to the surface like baby snakes slithering on the dry leaves.

As Dan continued to saw, more and more creepy looking worms wiggled from the ground. Vady began laughing and stepping away. She seemed so excited to see the mass of worms. But suddenly, she was breathing heavily and easing down at the base of a big oak tree. Dan looked around, and there she sat among the worms.

Knowing that something had gone horribly wrong, Dan dropped his saw and rushed to her side. He knelt down, put his arms around his wife, and she smiled. Tears welled in his eyes and for a moment he had no idea what to do. On that beautiful September morning just inside the woods near the crest of the hill behind their farm house, Maudy Nevady Walker had drawn her last breath. Learning against the base of the oak with a faint smile on her face, Vady died in the arms of the man she had loved for the majority of her life.

According to Dan, his first thought was to get her back to the house. Then he realized that he could not move her; therefore, Dan began yelling for help. He yelled and yelled, but no one answered. His mournful yells turned to grief stricken screams, but still no one came. Dan finally gave up and went to a neighbor's house to call for help and to notify his family.

By late afternoon, all family members, except Dan's youngest daughter Katie Lucille Walker, had been informed of Vady's passing. There was not quick or easy way to get a message to Vady's baby daughter at her home in Brindisi, Italy. After notifying the Red Cross and military authorities, the family expected that Lucy would be notified, but no word came of her notification. The family went ahead and buried the family matriarch.

Maudy Nevady (Vady) Legg Walker was laid to rest at Friendship Baptist Cemetery at Upshaw adjacent to the Old Jasper Road in Winston County, Alabama. The cemetery was referred to as Friendship on the Mountain. Vady's grave was near her young children that were buried years earlier. She had taken the homemade crepe flowers to the graves of her son James and her daughter Lora for so many years. Vady was buried next to those where over the years she had placed the homemade crepe paper flowers. All of Vady's children were present for the service except Katie Lucille Walker who was going about her daily life in Italy and did not know that her mother had died.

Knock on the Door

For several days, the death of her mother remained unknown to Katie Lucille, who was caring for her new baby boy. She was still recuperating from her terrifying escape from Tripoli, Libya. While she was still dealing with the very traumatic experience from war torn Libya, attempts were being made to let Katie Lucille know that her mother had passed away.

One morning days later while going about her usual daily task of preparing breakfast, getting children off to school, and changing baby diapers, there was a knock on her door. Asa had already gone to work. Lucy opened the door, and there stood two young soldiers. A very dangerous escape from the war torn country of Libya was still fresh on her mind when two young soldiers showed up at her door. She knew that the news was not good.

Katie Lucille's heart sank. She knew something terrible had happened. With regrets, the soldiers informed her that her mother had died several days before. Lucy was shocked. She was so heartbroken that she was unable to respond. Devastated by the news and a long way from her Alabama home where her mother had died, Lucy broke in to mournful sobbing and uncontrollable crying. Death had broken the strong bond she had with her loving mother.

Aunt Lucille told me, "I was back in Italy a little over three months when my mother died. It was days before I found out that my mother was dead! I found out after mother's funeral! I knew that it was no use trying to go back home because she was already buried. I would not get to see her one last time."

As Aunt Lucille was telling me of her mother's death, her voice trembled, her expression was sad, and tears welled up in her eyes and rolled down her cheeks. I could see that the pain was still there. It appeared that the scar on her heart was still not healed. Her memory of the news about the death of her mother was just as real as it was when she heard the devastating news from the two young soldiers.

Maudy Nevady Legg Walker died September 9, 1967. Her death occurred while Katie Lucille (Lucy) Walker and her family were stationed at the United States Air Force base near Brindisi, Italy. Lucy did not find out about her mother's death until days after she was already buried.

Katie Lucille had to deal with a terrible sadness at the loss of her dear mother; her grief ran deep. Lucy was a long way from the cotton fields of her hill country home in Alabama. Memories of her mother flashed across her mind time

142

and time again. Disappointed and deeply hurt, Katie Lucille realized that she must make a decision that she would never quite get over.

Shocked and grief stricken, Lucy bravely accepted the heartbreaking news. Yearning to see her mother's grave and talk to her daddy before his time, Lucy faced a heart wrenching decision. Leaving her family with a new born baby boy was not an option. Because of Asa's military security clearance and the top secret job, Lucy and her children would be allowed to go home, but she would have to leave her husband behind until he completed his tour of duty. She knew that it would be months before she would be reunited with her husband Asa if she left Italy to go home to Alabama.

Lucy knew she had to draw on that deep inner strength she had inherited from both her parents and to keep her life in perspective. Her young children needed her, and her husband expected her to be there to take care of their family. She knew there was nothing she could do for her mother now. Her mother was in her grave and that was all over. She would stay in Italy with her family until the next assignment stateside then she would show her last respects to her loving mother.

Going home was not a matter of desire or money. Because her mother was already buried, Katie Lucille would have to settle for paying tribute to her mother later by being the best mother she could be to her own children. Deep down, she was aware that going home again would never be the same.

People are transformed by the personal experiences they have, and Katie Lucille was no exception. She was the youngest of fourteen children, and as the baby of her family, she had a special bond with her mother. She always brought a smile to her mother's face, but for some fifteen years, Lucy had only gotten to see her mother about every three years. When she married Asa, Lucy had no idea that she would not be present for her mother's death and funeral. Her pain and agony could not be shared with her brothers and sisters.

More sacrifices than most people realize are demanded from a soldier's wife. Lucy had learned this through personal experience. Precious time away from family and friends could never be regained. Lucy knew that previous moments spent with her mother were only memories, and those too would fade with time but never be forgotten. That was her way of life and that was the way it would remain.

Italy had been such a beautiful place, but Katie Lucille's family had experienced more than their share of misfortunes shortly after they had arrived. Lucy's life threatening experience in Tripoli, Libya, when Roger was born was the most disturbing of all. Within a few weeks Cynthia had suffered a close call from chemical induced pneumonia. Then, there was the devastating news that Lucy's mother had died. All those incidents in such a short period of time had left Katie Lucille emotionally distraught. However just as they had done all their married life, she and Asa pulled together and were getting their life back on track when the news arrived that his new assignment would be Vietnam.

Chapter Sixteen

June 1968-Vietnam and San Antonio, Texas, USA

Within nine months of the death of Lucy's mother while the family was in Italy and just before Asa's tour of duty was to be completed, he was issued new orders for Vietnam. With war raging in Southeast Asia, it came as no surprise to Asa that his next tour of duty would be Vietnam.

The United States was involved in one of the most unpopular wars in its history. The Vietnam War had been rampant since its beginnings in 1957. The United States defended its involvement in the conflict on the grounds of being a deterrent to the spread of Communism. Communist forces in North Vietnam began attacking the South Vietnamese. As the conflict intensified, the United States intervened by sending numerous combat troops to support the South Vietnamese in 1965.

Asa was to report to Kelly Air Force Base near San Antonio, Texas, where he would leave his family while he was in Vietnam. Lucy said, "Asa had to go to Vietnam, and we could not go with him. We stayed at our home in San Antonio, Texas."

There was no option for Asa's family to follow him to Vietnam. Katie Lucille and the children family had to be assigned state side before Asa went to Vietnam. Therefore, Asa had to report for a third tour of duty at Kelly Air Force Base which was in June 1968 through September 30, 1970. For some sixteen years, Lucy and Asa had been together on all his tours of military duty, but Vietnam was different. She knew that she would be separated from her husband for two years and three months, except for a one week furlough for rest and recuperation.

After arriving back in the United Sates, Asa left his family for the first time of his military career. In order to maintain a quality living conditions, Lucy worked various jobs to supplement Asa's family income while he was in Vietnam. Katie Lucille became the primary caretaker of the family, and she began working as a waitress in the Villa Rama Restaurant. She would be responsible for taking care of their five children for the next two years.

Vietnam

During this assignment, Asa spent two years in Vietnam while Katie Lucille and the children lived near the base in Texas waiting on his return. Lucy said, "We arrived back at Kelly Air Force Base in San Antonio, Texas in June

1968. Shortly after we got back to the states, Asa went on his first one year tour in Vietnam."

Martha Jo said, "As soon we got back to Kelly Air Force Base, daddy went to Vietnam."

The tour of duty in Vietnam would be the first that Asa had not had his family by his side since he and Lucy had married. Asa most likely would not have stayed in the United States Air Force for twenty plus years had it not been for the support he received from his wife and his children. Katie Lucille and Martha Jo accompanied Asa to Alaska and back. Mark was born in Hartselle, Alabama, after Asa's hospitalization at Maxwell Air Force Base. Asa Lynn was born in Montgomery, Alabama. Katie Lucille, Martha Jo, Mark, and Asa Lynn accompanied Asa to Japan on their first foreign assignment. Cynthia was born in Maryland. Roger, their youngest, was their only child born on foreign soil. He came into this world in Tripoli, Libya.

No matter where Asa had been stationed his family was willing to go. Asa's children had never lived as civilians, so they did not realize the sacrifices that they were making. They were a patriotic family who loved their daddy. They had spent years traveling around the world from one duty station to another.

Lucy had been Asa's lifeline after his skiing accident in Alaska. She had convinced Asa's superiors to get a doctor who could repair his leg. Asa credited Lucy with saving not only his leg but also his military career. Now, he was going to the most controversial assignment that he had ever faced, and he would be going to Vietnam alone.

Before leaving for Vietnam, Asa made sure that his family was comfortably situated at his stateside assignment in Texas. When Asa went to Vietnam in June 1968, he had lived away from Alabama for over twenty years while serving with the United States military. But, Asa still considered Alabama his home, and he was always interested in hearing news about his childhood residence. He was especially concerned about events in North Alabama no matter where he was stationed. Asa had just returned from Italy prior to going to Vietnam, but he had kept up with developments in North Alabama.

The 1960's had been a period of transition for Alabama, but it was still considered a rural, poverty stricken, farming state. Few large cities including Birmingham, Huntsville, Montgomery, and Mobile were located in Alabama. The economic outlook was bleak, and industrial development was lacking. Public schools lagged behind. Alabama had gained a reputation of being backward and segregated place to live. In spite of its reputation, Asa Walker was proud to be from the State of Alabama. Asa was always interested in talking to other soldiers from Alabama especially when he was away from his family in Vietnam.

Asa had been stationed at Maxwell Air Force Base in Montgomery, Alabama. So when the 1965 Selma to Montgomery voting rights march attracted national attention, Asa was anxious to hear first hand from fellow soldiers who had been in Alabama. However, in the desolate jungles of Vietnam, Asa had not met many people from his home State of Alabama.

An Alabama Boy

One day during the early summer of 1970 in the central highlands at Pleiku Air Force Base in Vietnam, Asa Walker found himself conversing with a young airman who mentioned that he was from Alabama. The young man had been drafted, and he joined the United States Air Force shortly after his high school graduation. As it turned out, Curtis Ramsey (Mike) O'Neal, Jr. was from Lawrence County, Alabama.

Coincidentally, Asa was from the adjoining Morgan County . Asa had grown up in Hartselle, Alabama, and he had been in the military for over twenty three years. Mike had lived some thirty miles west of Hartselle in Mt. Hope. The small tight knit community was about ten miles west of Moulton, Alabama. Mike had lived in Mt. Hope, and he had graduated from Mt. Hope High School before joining the military.

In the course of the conservation between Asa Walker and Mike O'Neal, Mike mentioned to Asa that there were Walkers who lived near Mt. Hope and that there was a girl in his class named June Walker. Now, that was such a coincidence because June Walker was Asa's niece. June was the daughter of Lucy's brother Brady Walker.

Little else about their conservation was ever revealed. Asa never mentioned whether or not he and Mike discussed the Selma to Montgomery voting rights march, but they did talk about their home state, Alabama. Asa did mention to Mike that he was planning to retire when this second tour of duty in Vietnam was completed.

According to Mike, at some point a missile hit the hooch that Asa, Mike, and fellow troops used as living quarters. The hooch also housed their supplies and the bunks where they slept. The projectile destroyed the open air building and shredded the beds where they slept. Thankfully, the rocket hit during the day while the soldiers were not in their bunks. On that particular occasion, both Asa and Mike avoided injury. Others were not so lucky!

After the destruction of their hooch, Asa and Mike did not see each other again. Although their meeting was brief, they remembered each other long after the Vietnam War. Asa and Mike's path never crossed again.

When Mike returned to Mt. Hope, Alabama, he visited his Alma Mater, Mt. Hope High School where June Walker Reed was teaching. Mike told June about meeting her Uncle Asa Walker while he was in Vietnam. June immediately called her dad Brady Walker with the news concerning Mike and Asa meeting.

None of the extended family members knew where Asa served during his military service in Vietnam. Family members knew that Asa was serving two tours of duty in Vietnam, but had no idea about the location of his duty station. Thanks to Mike O'Neal, the family learned that Asa was in the central highlands at Pleiku Air Force Base while he was in Vietnam on his second tour of duty.

When Asa returned home after completing his second tour in Vietnam, he recalled meeting one of June Walker Reed's high school classmates by the name of Mike O'Neal. Since Asa and Mike served together in Vietnam, Asa wanted to know if Mike had lived through the war to make it home. Thankfully, both Mike and Asa had survived their traumatic ordeal of military service during the Vietnam War.

Following his tour of duty in Vietnam, Mike was stationed in Italy. Mike's wife Helen Steele O'Neal was allowed to accompany him on that tour of duty. It is ironic both Mike and Asa served together with Asa going to Vietnam from Italy and Mike going from Vietnam to Italy. Both Asa and Mike were honorably discharged from the United States Air Force. Today, Mike and Helen live in Memphis, Tennessee.

Vietnam Soldier Sacrifices

Sadly to say, other family members and friends of Asa and Mike gave their lives for their country while serving with the United States armed forces in the Vietnam War. A total of 58,220 United States soldiers paid the ultimate sacrifice; they died in the far away land and jungles of Vietnam.

A large number of young Americans expressed opposition to the war in Vietnam especially after the draft was reinstated. Many of the brave men, who fought and did their duty during the Vietnam War, returned home to a thankless nation.

At that time of the Vietnam War being a veteran was not popular and for many soldiers who returned home the reception was anything but welcoming. Although the United States never declared war in Vietnam, countless American soldiers lost their lives. Most of the soldiers who came back home were forever changed; Asa was no exception.

Most people do not truly understand the sacrifices made by veterans and their families, but because of their contributions, America has remained a free country. Countless ordinary men and women have served in the armed forces of the United States, and some have been recognized for their service. Some soldiers have been acknowledged for their achievements, and they have gone on to receive national acclaim.

Many other soldiers simply returned home with wounds both physical and mental from which they never recovered. Numerous others made the ultimate sacrifice. Veterans have experienced and array of reactions for their service. They were not all heroes of combat; their role was not one that gained national attention, but people will never know what would have happened if they had not been at their duty stations.

Another Knock

After Asa was in Vietnam for one year, he got one week of military leave called rest and recuperation to be with his wife. Lucy said, "Asa was in Vietnam for one year before he got a leave. During his leave, we met in Honolulu, Hawaii, for one week. I decided to make his week one that he would not forget. I bought five different colored wigs and different outfits to go with each one. Every day that Asa and I were in Hawaii, I dressed as a different woman; we just had a great time. I knew when he went back to Vietnam for another year that I may or may not ever see him again. After we spent a week in Hawaii, Asa went back to Vietnam for another year, and I went back to Kelly Air Force Base in Texas."

After being with Asa in Hawaii, Katie Lucille Walker returned to her children in San Antonio, Texas. Shortly after she got home, two young military men wearing their dress uniforms came to her door. Lucy responded to a knock. Her heart pounded wildly as she opened the door. She knew that something terrible had happened. She knew that death had again made a call, but for whom? One of the young soldiers regrettable informed her that her daddy, Monroe Daniel Walker, had passed away on October 2, 1969. She was immediately relieved that her husband Asa Walker was not a casualty of the Vietnam War, but she felt extreme sadness and grief that she had lost her daddy.

Since she was at Kelly Air Force Base in San Antonia, Texas, with her children, Lucy would be able to go to Alabama for her father's funeral. Attending her mother's funeral was a privilege that Lucy missed, but she would make the trip to pay her last respects to her daddy. All Lucy's brothers and sisters that had lived to adulthood were at the funeral services for their daddy.

Dan Walker was buried at Friendship on the Mountain at Upshaw adjacent to the Indian trail called the Old Jasper Road. He was laid to rest beside his wife Miss Vady in the cemetery located not far from the nearby Corinth Community where they had married at some sixty two years earlier.

That October gathering for the funeral of their father would be the last time that all ten of the Walker siblings would be together at the same time and place. Little did the brothers and sisters know that the next family gathering would be to attend one of their funerals. Over the next few years, the siblings would gather to say their last farewells to a brother or a sister.

Top L-R: Ida, Roy, Thurman, Violene, Oliver, Lodean, Paul
Kneeling L-R: Kenneth, Lucille, Brad

At the time of Dan's death, Lucy was living in Texas, and Asa Walker was in Vietnam. After her father's funeral, Lucille went back to her Texas home. She would not return to Alabama until Asa came home from Vietnam and her oldest daughter Martha Jo graduated from high school.

Asa served in peacetime during the Cold War at the end of World War II, during the Korean War, and in the undeclared Vietnam War. Although he was not serving on the front lines, Asa was often in life and death situations. Like most soldiers who served in war torn countries, Asa faced various traumatic situations. The long term psychological effects of his service would not be obvious until after he returned home from Vietnam.

Immediately after completing his two year tour in Vietnam, Asa came back home to his wife and children at Kelly Air Force Base the last day of September in 1970, and he retired the next day. One of the reasons for his early retirement was his daughter Martha Jo Walker had just started in the eleventh grade in public school at San Antonio, Texas, and she was not going to another military assignment.

Martha Jo said, "I started in the ninth grade in the public school which was South San Antonio High School. I stayed in school until I graduated in 1972. With some of my teachers, I stayed in trouble all the time because they were not teaching the history that I had actually experienced. When they were talking about the Berlin Wall being built, I said wait a minute. I always objected to some of the wrong things I was taught. They told me, we do not want American children to know what is going on overseas. There were 1,973 in my graduating class; only about two hundred fifty spoke English and the rest talked in Spanish."

Another reason for Asa's retirement mentioned by his immediate family members was that Asa had changed. It appeared to some that he suffered from post traumatic stress disorder because of his service in the war torn Vietnam.

Asa was confronted with a sincere dilemma when he returned home from Vietnam. He faced and undesirable alternative. He would have to go to Germany by himself or he would have to retire from the United States Air Force where he had planned on a thirty year career. For Asa, it was a "no brainer," he would retire.

Without question, his family was more important than his military career. The real life consequences of his decision would play out in a way that no one would have guessed. In the days following his retirement, Asa would become more and more dependent on his wife Katie Lucille and more and more demanding of his children.

Chapter Seventeen

After Military Service

Katie Lucille (Lucy) Walker had followed her military husband all around the world on their great adventure as he served in the United States Air Force. After coming home from serving two years in Vietnam, Asa's military service was over, and he retired on October 1, 1970. Lucy said, "Asa retired from the military after spending twenty four years, two months, and five days on active duty."

On September 30, 1970, Asa returned to Texas after spending two full years of duty in Vietnam. The next day on October 1, 1970, Asa retired from the military career he had chosen as a young man. Lucy said, "When Asa finally come home to Texas, he had already been reassigned to Germany. Asa had planned to stay thirty years in the military, but when he came back from Vietnam, the Air Force had already cut orders for him to go back to Germany. Jo was in high school in San Antonio, Texas, and she told us that she was not going back to Germany on tour with the family."

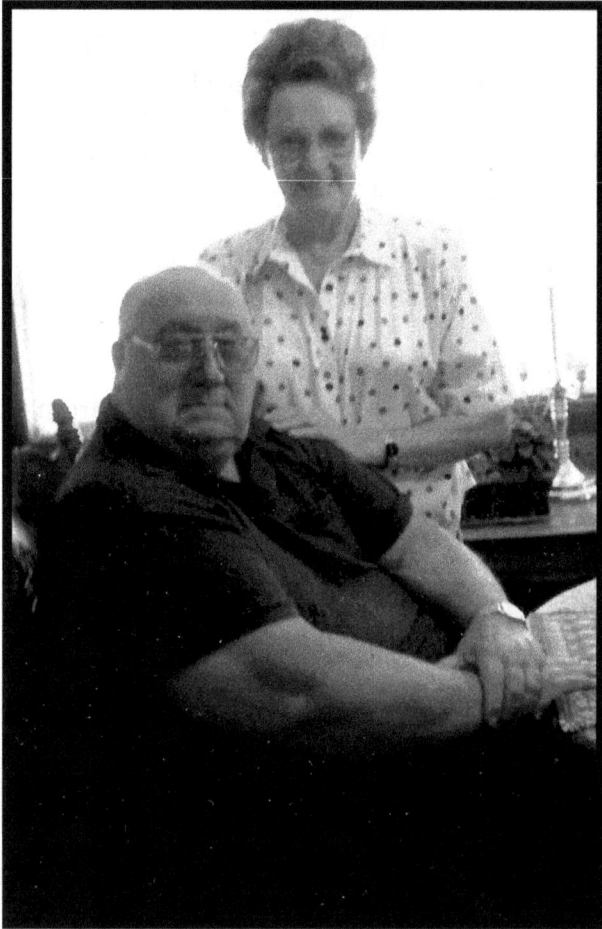

Asa and Lucille Walker

According to Lucy, "Jo did not have a place she could really call home; therefore, she never developed a deep love for a home place like people that live in one place all their lives. My three oldest children did not develop permanent friendships with strong bonds. When they were small, we were moving all the time and no place really felt like home to them." When the Walker family moved to Texas for the second time, they began to feel that they had gotten home. But Lucy would eventually feel those deep family roots pull on her heart strings for her childhood home of Alabama.

"For a long time, the only place that Jo developed roots and felt like it was home was in San Antonio, Texas, where she graduated from high school in 1972. Jo had been everywhere and never had any friends from childhood up and none of my kids had regular friends. We had already served a tour in Germany and Jo was in school; she was not going back to Germany," stated Lucy.

Asa said, "I have been two years by myself in Vietnam, and if y'all are not going with me, I will just retire." Asa loved the military, but he loved his family much more. For two long years, he had no idea if he would ever see his family again. Those were the two most agonizing years that Asa had ever lived, and he was not about to endure three more years away from his family.

Asa did not hesitate about retirement from the military even though he had planned on staying for thirty years. He did not give it a second thought when he found out that his family would not accompany him to Germany. Without any hesitation, Asa decided that his military career would terminate immediately as soon as he could sign the paper work.

Martha Jo said, "I believe daddy was mentally affected while serving in Vietnam, and he carried those scars the rest of his life. He served two tours of duty in Vietnam through 1968 to 1969; then he had two weeks leave in Hawaii! He went back to Vietnam from 1969 to 1970. He returned to the states at Kelly Air Force Base, in San Antonio, Texas, on September 30, 1970, and he retired one day later on October 1, 1970!"

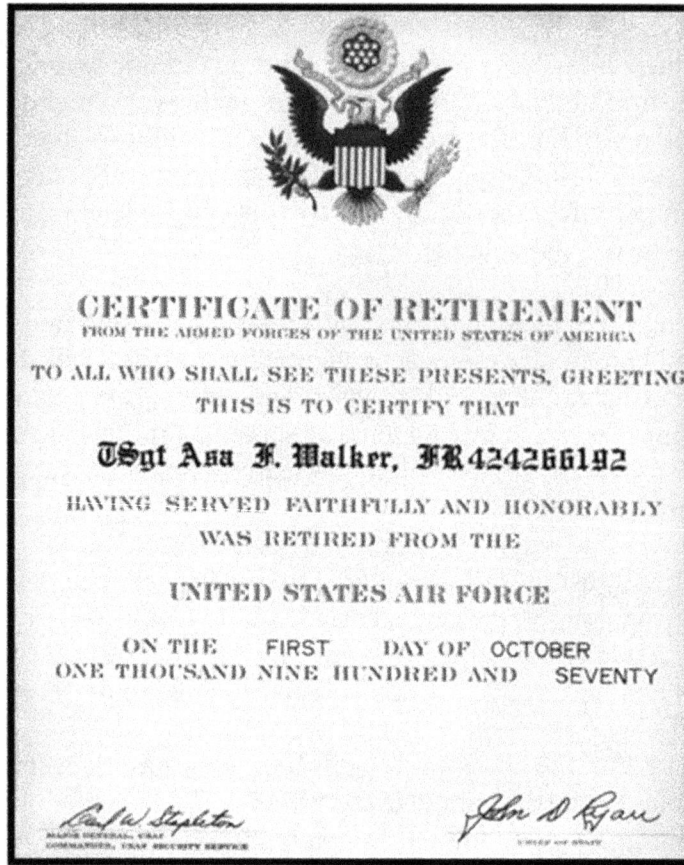

CERTIFICATE OF RETIREMENT
FROM THE ARMED FORCES OF THE UNITED STATES OF AMERICA

TO ALL WHO SHALL SEE THESE PRESENTS, GREETING
THIS IS TO CERTIFY THAT

TSgt Asa F. Walker, FR424266192

HAVING SERVED FAITHFULLY AND HONORABLY
WAS RETIRED FROM THE

UNITED STATES AIR FORCE

ON THE   FIRST   DAY OF OCTOBER
ONE THOUSAND NINE HUNDRED AND   SEVENTY

The great military adventure and world tour that Asa and Lucy had started as a young married couple came to an abrupt end. Lucy had dreamed of seeing the world, but orders were for Germany. That place brought terrible memories of brutal deaths. Now it appeared that Lucy's family would adjust to being in one place in the United States, but in her heart, deep roots were pulling her back to the hills and those old cotton fields of her youth.

Martha Jo continued, "When his boots hit the ground in American, I told him I was not going to another tour in Germany and he said he was retiring."

Returning home was a wonderful experience but assimilating into society was not as easy as it would appear to civilians. As with other Vietnam veterans, Asa had concerns about finding a job that would enable him to support his family.

156

He had to recoup and deal with the mental, emotional, and social aspects of returning to civilian life.

In some areas of the country, veterans returning from Vietnam were referred to as 'Baby Killers,' some were spit on, and others were refused to be accepted as heros. Many times, the general public failed to realize the huge price and sacrifice that Vietnam veterans and their families had paid in their effort to assure our freedoms. The soldier's personal sacrifices in the jungles of Vietnam were as horrible as any war. Thousands of these young men paid the ultimate sacrifice, and many families still mourn their loss. Thank goodness the attitude of the vast majority of Americans has changed since Vietnam, and today, most veterans are considered heros.

Family members could tell that two years in Vietnam had caused a dramatic change in Asa Walker's personality. Jo said, "We knew that he was suffering from some mental issues, but at the time people did not know what it was called. We later learned about post traumatic stress which they label today as PTSD! Daddy would become very irritable and start yelling."

Asa's usual mild mannered nature had slipped away and he became much more irritable. Asa could be stern man with his family, but after Vietnam, he at times would become almost a tyrant. After his military retirement, he seemed to become demanding, and Lucy was at his beckoning call.

At times, Asa was seemingly out of control emotionally. He could not stop his insatiable eating habits. Even though he had always been somewhat heavy, his eating became excessive leading to tremendous weight gain. Asa probably tried to deal with the stress of his service through a compulsive eating disorder which led to excessive weight gain that eventually resulted in his inability to work. His condition would result in social security disability.

Martha Jo continued, "Even though he had weight issues while on various tours of duty, his eating habits got much worse after Vietnam. I think he turned to food as an outlet to the post traumatic stress he was experiencing. Eventually because of his weigh, daddy was placed on social security disability in June 1983. By the time he died on February 24, 1999, daddy weighed about 525 pounds." Asa's eating issues led to disability after his retirement from the military.

In an effort to keep her daughter happy and allow her to be able to graduate from a school that felt like home, Lucy and her family would spend nearly two more years in San Antonio, Texas. Katie Lucille and Asa worked in Texas and waited until their oldest daughter Martha Jo Walker graduated from high school in 1972.

Eventually the family would head back to the Alabama home of Lucy's birth. Shortly after Martha Jo graduated from high school, the family of Asa and Katie Lucille packed their belongings and headed east. Lucy said, "We moved back to Morgan County, Alabama, on July 30, 1972."

With the career in the military over Asa and Lucy became very competitive sales people. While living in Texas, they begin selling mobile homes, and during their first year, they won a two week European tour. Katie Lucille and Asa realized that hard work had enabled them to continue their world tour and the great adventure they had started as a young married couple. For the first time in many years, the military husband and soldier's wife could travel together on a great European vacation; their hard work was paying off.

Martha Jo Walker Wise said, "Shortly after retiring from the military, daddy and mother started selling mobile homes in San Antonio, Texas. During the first year, they sold over one million dollars of mobile homes and won a ten day trip on the Rhine River in Europe. During the tour, they visited nine different countries."

All her life, Katie Lucille Walker had been very competitive in everything she attempted. Selling mobile homes was no different because of her ambition to always be the best. During their second year in the mobile home sales, the couple won another trip to Europe. Again, they got to see and enjoy a part of the world that they had never visited. Lucy's dream of seeing places far from the cotton fields of North Alabama had come true.

Martha Jo said, "The next year, they sold one and a half million dollars of mobile homes. For their efforts, they won a trip to Belgium, Holland, and Switzerland." After all the tours of military duty in many different countries, the couple was finally getting to have paid vacations with each other. Their dedicated work ethic was paying dividends, and they were enjoying having fun with each other visiting foreign countries places without being on duty and having to report to military bases.

Chapter Eighteen

Sweet Home Alabama

Asa and his wife were hard working people in San Antonio, Texas. In addition to selling mobile homes, Katie Lucille worked in a restaurant. The couple was very successful, but something seemed to be missing in Lucy's life. As a young girl, she had developed deep roots in the red clay of North Alabama and now she wanted to go home. She had the desire to live the rest of her life near the place she called home while growing up; therefore, shortly after her daughter Martha Jo graduated from high school, Katie Lucille brought her family back to the only area she considered home.

Martha Jo said, "After I graduated from high school on May 26, 1972, daddy made the trip to Alabama to find us a home. Mom sold our house in San Antonio, Texas, and packed all of our belongings in one week. We drove three cars with trailers containing all our stuff and came home to Alabama. After six months in Alabama, I moved back to Texas and stayed there for two years before I decided that I wanted to be closer to mother and daddy."

Martha Jo Walker had moved ever few months of her life until she went back to San Antonio, Texas, during the two years her father was in Vietnam; therefore, she only developed roots in Texas. Jo was reluctant to leave Texas after her graduation because it felt like home and where she should be. At first, she intended to return to Texas and stay there the rest of her life, but family ties finally called her back to Alabama.

After returning to Alabama, Lucy returned to a familiar way of life. Her immediate family had lived in the same area for over sixty years. She had grown up on the family farm located about a mile from the home where she would live her remaining days. Being gone some twenty years away from the cotton fields of her birthplace, Katie Lucille Walker returned to an Alabama that was totally different than the one she knew for the first eighteen years of her life.

Lucy soon realized that things were different. Both her parents were dead, her childhood friends were gone or had families of their own, and the rest of her siblings had lost the parents that had pulled them together in the past. Lucy knew her decision to travel with her husband had impacted her children who had missed out on family activities. She knew things could not make up for years gone by, and she was not ready to start with parties.

Katie Lucille said, "When we come back to Morgan County, Alabama, all my friends were married and had children, and I was married to Asa Walker. When we got this mobile home and moved in, people told us they were going to give us a house warming. I said no! I never had a baby shower, my children never had a birthday party, and I never had anything like that, and you are not going to give me a house warming party. I did not have it for my kids, and I am not going to have one for our house. We will make it; we got it covered honey. It is amazing how people have showers, but we never had the opportunity while we were with the military."

Shortly after returning to Morgan County, Alabama, Asa and Katie Lucille purchased a house site next to her sister Ida who lived on the north side of Highway 157. The home place was just one mile west from the intersection of Highways 41 and 157 which was in sight of Lucy's childhood home. Asa and Lucy moved a double wide mobile home on the site and lived there until both passed away.

Finally Katie Lucille was back at sweet home Alabama. There was no one happier to see his baby sister return home than her brother Brady Walker. According to Lucille, one of her favorite brothers was Brady; they always challenged each other when picking cotton. In nearly all photographs of the family, Katie Lucille and Brady were always pictured beside each other. It was obvious that Brady loved his baby sister and that she love him. Both Katie Lucille and Brady had an extrovert personality and never met a stranger. They could talk to anyone they met like they had been friends for years.

In all of the times they were together during visits, I never heard Brady and Aunt Lucille having but one disagreement or argument. The only difference in opinions between Aunt Lucille and Brady was when she moved from Texas back to Alabama after Asa retired from the military. Aunt Lucille decided to buy and live in a doublewide mobile home which she planned to move to the piece of land on Highway 157 that she had purchased from her older sister Ida Walker Armbrester.

Since Aunt Ida lived in a nice home next door to Katie Lucille's property, Brady wanted his little sister to build a brick house. Since Asa and Lucille had sold mobile homes in Texas, and also shortly after they moved to Alabama, they were very comfortable buying a double wide mobile home. Lucy made it clear to Brady what she wanted and that was the end of the discussion.

For as long as Brady lived, Aunt Lucille would visit him just about once a week. On or about May 26 of every year after she returned to Alabama, Aunt Lucille always showed up at Brady and Novel's house with a fresh strawberry pie. My Aunt Lucille and my mother Novel Wilburn Walker shared the same day of birth on May 26. Lucy would celebrate their mutual birthdays with her famous strawberry pie that my mother loved so well. After my mother's death, the strawberry pies were too painful to bring to my dad's house. Neither my Aunt Lucille nor my dad needed to be reminded of great times gone by.

In Alabama, Asa and Lucy continued to sell mobile homes for about two more years. During this time, Asa got so overweight that he was placed on disability; working became very difficult for him. Since Asa's military retirement and disability check did not provide enough money for the family to meet all their financial obligations and live comfortably, Lucy worked to earn extra money.

For a short time, my Aunt Lucille worked in a garment factory for my mother Novel Walker. She also sewed tailor made clothes for individuals. She was an excellent seamstress who had learned to sew as a young girl. One particular young woman who participated in beauty pageants often hired her to create pageant dresses. Lucy spent many hours painstakingly stitching sequins and rhinestones on ball gowns and formal dresses.

Katie Lucille's mother taught her to sew, and after Lucy married, she made her own clothes. She continued to sew after she had children of her own, and she made clothes for them. Her first child was a girl, and Lucy sewed fancy little dresses for her baby, Martha Jo. After her son Mark was born, she made rompers for him to match Jo's dresses. Then Lynn came along, and all three children often wore matching outfits. When Cynthia and Roger made their appearances the older children were no longer willing to wear matching outfits.

Later, Katie Lucille started working as a waitress at Gerald's Restaurant on Highway 31 in Decatur, Alabama. Gerald Mack Payne owned the eating establishment and was the nephew of Lucy and the son of Lucy's sister Ida. Lucy had experience working in restaurants; in fact, her very first job after graduating from high school was in a restaurant with Ida's daughter Billie Sue. After working at Gerald's Restaurant for a few years, Katie Lucille got a job at Demco where she worked as a secretary.

Chapter Nineteen

Avon Calling

In her spare time and off days between work and church, Katie Lucille enjoyed going to yard sales looking for items that could be bought at a reasonable cost and that her family could use. One day when she stopped at a yard sale, a door of opportunity opened to the outgoing soldier's wife. As she was looking for yard sale bargains in October 1987, she met an Avon lady by the name of Mary Long. Ms. Long and Lucy got to chatting and eventually became great friends.

That day at the yard sell, Mary Long realized that Katie Lucille never met a stranger. Mary decided to tell Lucy about the company that she worked for and invite Lucy to consider selling Avon products. Lucy was excited to hear more about the Avon business. After being fully informed on the company and their products, Katie Lucille agreed to start selling Avon door to door. She was always looking for ways to improve her family situation and lifestyle, and this seemed to be a perfect fit.

Even though Lucy was actively working and going to church on a regular basis, she accepted the role as the primary bread winner because Asa retirement was not enough and he was not able to hold a full time job. Although he received a decent retirement, money was tight. A few years after Asa retired from the Air Force, his health declined. Asa was declared disable by the Social Security Administration; therefore, it fell on Lucy to supplement their income. Asa had spent much of his time at home in his recliner. Aunt Lucille pointed to the chair and said, "Asa spent most of his last fifteen years sitting right there."

Since Asa was disabled, he was more than willing to promote his wife because he knew that she had stood by his side in turbulent places around the world. This time, he would support her as they started another adventure together. Asa worked hard to make the Avon business a very successful career for his wife because she had done the same for him.

Therefore, at an age when most people were looking to retire, Lucy embarked on a new career selling Avon. It allowed Lucy to meet new people and meeting people was something she enjoyed. At the same time, she was able to bring home some extra money. She had experience in sales and being an Avon representative offered her an opportunity to earn money as well as providing her the flexible schedule she needed.

Selling Avon products was a big step, but turned out to be a wonderful journey where Lucy touched so many lives in a lot of different ways. Inspired by her love for people and her desire to stay active in her community, she found satisfaction in helping others become more self-confident and self-supporting. Lucy realized that every sale was a chance to meet someone who could introduce her to another customer. Her networking soon paid off in big benefits.

Lucy's first year of selling Avon began in the fall of 1987. During the first few months of her start up year, she sold over $10,000.00 worth of Avon products. The fiscal year of the Avon business ran from March of one year to March of the next year. After her success with the initial sales, Katie Lucille encouraged her oldest daughter Martha Jo to assist her with the Avon business. Jo agreed to work with her mother as an Avon sales person.

In April 1988, Lucy and Jo attended an Avon meeting at the Airport Sheraton in Huntsville, Alabama; the event had over 400 people in attendance. Lucy and Jo were setting near the stage because they were honoring Lucy for her first year of sales. The speaker asked who wanted to go to the Bahamas for selling a minimum of $110,000.00 worth of Avon products during one year.

Jo said, "We were sitting next to the stage because momma was being honored for her high sales. Not knowing any better, when the question was asked, mom and I raised our hands and we got real excited. I looked around, and we were the only two people in that huge room that were holding up their hands; we felt kind of stupid."

Jo continued, "A few days later, our first district manager of Avon Judy Hale came to a meeting at mom and dad's house. She talked to mom, dad, and me about different ideas about how to reach our goal of the $110,000.00 in sales for the year. Mom got our Avon books, and we put our hands over them and prayed that if it be God's will that we would reach our goal for the year."

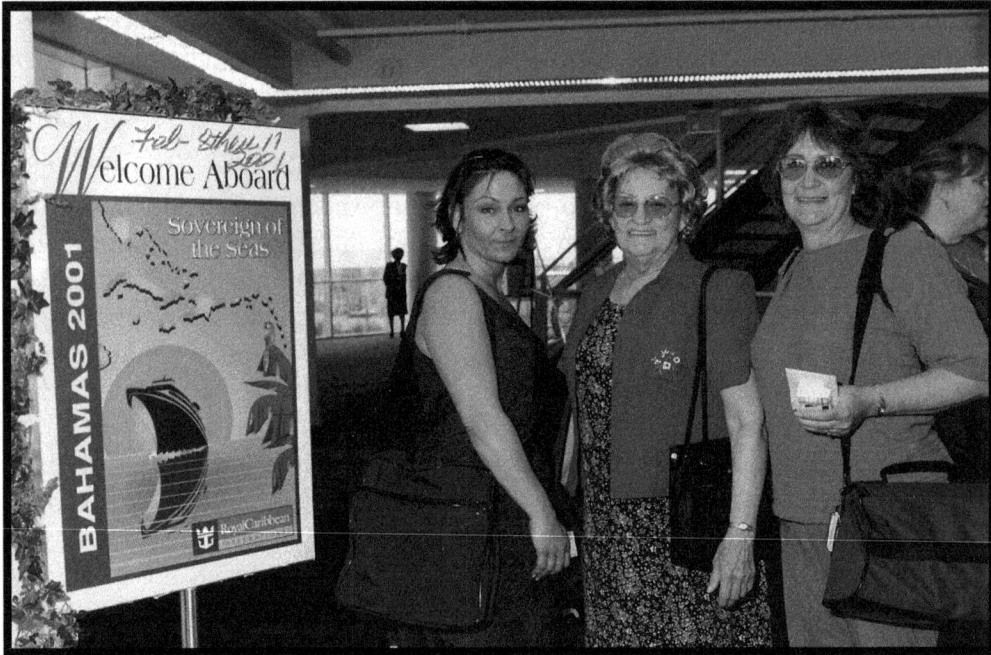
Cynthia, Katie Lucille, and Jo on Avon trip to Bahamas 2/8-11/2001

Not only did Judy Hale convince Lucy and Jo that they could reach the high goal they had set for themselves, but she also convinced Asa to become actively involved in his wife's success. Asa agreed to do everything that he could because he knew that his wife had supported him throughout his military career and did everything in her power to promote him. Asa accepted the challenge and probably figured that turn about was fair play. Now he was in a position to help his wife become successful, and he did.

Jo said, "Judy told daddy that he should be real proud of his wife and help her be the 'Best of the Best' seller of the year. Daddy became the secretary for momma. He learned the Avon books cover to cover, and he learned everything he could about new customers. He answered the phone, chatted with clients, and set up appointments." Asa took the reins and charged ahead. He promoted the Avon products and supported his wife as she had done for him.

Top Seller at Site 2010-2011

Lucy Walker

District 1140

$114,587

Congratulations & thank you!
Sherri Mauter
Camellia Division Sales Manager

AVON
President's
Recognition Program

Martha Jo said, "Daddy took Avon orders by phone, helped sell new Avon products. He recorded addresses and phone numbers, and wrote orders. He would learn things about our customers and talk to them about their kids, animals, and anything they wanted to discuss. Daddy was extremely important in helping mother get off to a great start with Avon."

With a combined effort of Asa, Lucy, and Martha Jo, they reached the goal they set. Jo said, "We did it; by March of 1989, we passed our goal of $110,000.00 in Avon sales. Momma reached beyond that amount of sales for the next twenty six years."

Sadly Asa Francis Walker, Jr. passed away on February 24, 1999, but he did live to see his wife become a very successful business woman. Asa had a major role in her achievement. Katie Lucille Walker had stood by her man during his military career, and he stood by her to become the Best of the Best Avon representatives.

President's Recognition Program

Best Seller Recognition

LUCY WALKER

District 1136
Camellia Division
2011-2012

#2	JEWELRY	$13,889
#3	COLOR	$16,851
#3	GIFTS	$ 2,274
#6	MARK	$ 2,531
#9	PERSONAL CARE	$11,384
#10	SKIN CARE	$ 8,328
#13	SKIN SO SOFT	$ 3,510
#15	FRAGRANCE	$12,952

    Uncle Asa (Ace) Francis Walker, Jr. was carried to Friendship Baptist Cemetery at Upshaw in Winston County, Alabama, to be buried. He was the son of Asa Francis Walker, Sr. and Leatha Bell Scott Walker. Asa was the brother of Lewis Luther Walker, Nora Bell Bourgeois, and Martha Cleo White. Asa was a Technical Sergeant with the United States Air Force, and he was credited with service during World War II, Korean War, and Vietnam War.

    After the death of her soldier Asa, Lucy continued selling over $110,000.00 worth of Avon products for the next fifteen years. She won three fully paid trips to the Bahamas, three trips to Hawaii, and two trips to Alaska. These trips were usually cruises and were fully paid for by Avon. In addition, Lucy won free fully paid trips to New Orleans, New York, San Francisco, Puerto Vallarta, Puerto Rico, Cancun, and many other places.

    Aunt Lucille told me, "I won so many trips with Avon that I got tired of going." Katie Lucille had been all over the world during her husband's military career. Traveling ever year, even though it was an honor, was tiring. As Aunt

Lucille got older and after her husband died, her deep family roots held her near the old cotton fields of her Morgan County home; therefore, she started letting her two daughters go on the fully paid trips that she had won for her high sales in Avon.

Jo said, "Of the twenty six years mother spent with Avon, seventeen of those years were in a leadership role in network marketing with the company. There were six levels within the Avon Corporation. The top or inner circle of Avon was level six with sales over $220,000.00. My mother was in level five which was over $110,000 in sales."

Martha Jo contributes much of that success to the fact that her mother would always take the new Avon books she received and pray over them. She backed up those reverent prayers with the hard work that she had known all her life. It was not by accident that Katie Lucille was a successful business and sales lady. She believed in the power of prayer and applied that to her Avon business.

She also put tremendous amounts of energy and time at being the best at everything she attempted, and Avon was no different.

Over the twenty six years Lucy was with Avon, she received numerous awards and recognitions for her high sales. She also won cruises to many beautiful places around the United States. Until the year she died, Katie Lucille Walker was among the "Best of the Best" in the Avon business.

Chapter Twenty

Katie Lucille's Children

Asa and Lucy were determined to maintain a close family unit even though Asa's career required them to move from one assignment to another in strange places around the world. Little did they realize the long term impact it would have their children. Their older children would live very convoluted lives on their journey to becoming young adults before they would land somewhere permanent.

The three older children Martha Jo, Mark, and Asa Lynn lived at so many different addresses that they were unable to remember all of them. They grew up living in apartments, rental houses, base housing, and sometimes a house their parents had bought, but they moved from country to country every year to three years or more often. They were exposed to a diverse mix of people and to the complex cultural heritage of the foreign countries where they lived.

Unlike many of their peers who had spent their entire childhoods in one place, Katie Lucille's older children never stayed in one place long enough to put down roots. They would never have childhood friends with whom they would graduate high school and go off to college. They were not a part of big family gathering such as Easter, Thanksgiving, or Christmas, nor were they able to celebrate with childhood friends, cousins, relatives, and other extended family members at school functions, birthdays parties, wedding, or other common social gathering that so many take for granted. This was not to say that they did not develop friendships, but their friends were always left behind when they had move to another location. People walked into their lives for short periods of time and moved on to never be heard from again. Of course, some would stay in touch for a few years but eventually fade into a memory of another place and another time.

Cell phones and computers were not readily available when Katie Lucille's children were growing up, so long distance friendships were few and rarely maintain for long periods of time. Therefore, Asa and Lucy's children grew up as 'military brats' a term used to refer to the children of serving members of the armed forces.

No matter where they were, Katie Lucille engulfed herself and her children in the culture and history of the particular duty station to which Asa was assigned. As a result, her children received a broad based education far beyond that found in books. Although they usually lived in off base housing, the three older children were educated on base in military schools in foreign countries.

The three older children did not feel the same sense of place in the small rural towns of North Alabama that were so familiar to their mother and father. Their lives were much more transit. Yet, Lucy's children, who had traveled the world, would eventually find their sense of place. They too would put down roots in the foothills to the Warrior Mountains of North Alabama not far from the cotton fields of the childhood home of their mother.

Originally, Asa expected to be with his wife and children through a thirty year military career, but life presented unscheduled changes. Several factors contributed to a change in the direction that the family was traveling. First, Berlin, Germany, was a bad experience for the young family, and Asa last orders were for another tour in Germany. Second, Tripoli, Libya, caused grave concern for the family's safety. Third, the death of her mother while in Italy left unhealed scars on Lucy. Fourth, during the two year term of separation during Asa's Vietnam tour, he had to leave his beloved wife to care for babies, pre-teens, and a teenager which put a great deal of stress on the entire family. Fifth, Asa and Lucy's consideration for all their children to have a stable life brought an end to a fascinating military career that spanned some twenty four years.

By the time Asa and Lucy left Italy, they had five children. Now with five children who they wanted to develop family roots and a feeling of home, Katie Lucille and Asa decided that they had dedicated enough of their lives to the military. With their decision to live as civilians, the globetrotting military family moved back to within a mile of where Katie Lucille (Lucy) Walker had been born.

Katie Lucille's life as a soldier's wife had gone full circle. She left the cotton fields of her childhood home with nine brothers and sisters living to old age. She and her children had lived her dream of traveling to countries around the globe. She had faced near death situations in Berlin and Tripoli. She returned to where her family roots had grown deep as a child.

Eventually, all of Katie Lucille's children moved within a short distance of her home, and they were able to visit their mother on a regular basis. Lucy had lost her mother, father, and all her siblings, but she was blessed with eleven grandchildren and fifteen great grandchildren. During her life, Lucy was gifted with many offspring as a legacy to her and her military husband Asa.

Katie Lucille's daughter Martha Jo Walker Wise had a baby girl named Heather; Lucy's first grandchild. She was a beautiful little girl that was born with severe medical problems which were ironically tied to military service. Heather's father was a Vietnam veteran who had been exposed to Agent Orange. Heather had been born with spinal bifida and was a hydrocephalic baby.

It is estimated that some eighty five percent of the Vietnam soldiers exposed to Agent Orange had babies with the same type of medical problems. Martha Jo Walker Wise said, "If Heather had lived long enough, we would have been eligible for compensation for medical bills and expenses because of her father's exposure to Agent Orange, but she died before we were able to file for coverage of her medical costs. I lost two more babies and both had spinal bifida. After having three pregnancies with the same results, we decided not to try to have any children."

At her home near the old cotton fields a long way from Berlin and Tripoli, Katie Lucille begin to enjoy the simple things in life with her children by her side. She loved her children and grandchildren and enjoyed having them at her home to celebrate all their birthdays, holidays, and special events. Her children also enjoyed being with their mother on her birthday.

Because of her love for family and God, Lucy conducted herself in a way that her children, grandchildren, great grandchildren, and relatives would always look up to her and be proud of her accomplishments in life. On May 26, 2008, Katie Lucille Walker celebrated her seventy fifth birthday with her children Asa Lynn, Roger, Mark, Martha Jo, and Cynthia.

Katie Lucille's life had become much more stable with children, grandchildren, and great grandchildren that lived nearby. She became focused on family, church, and her Avon business. Her two daughters Martha Jo and Cynthia were eager to help their mother; however, it would not be long until the tables would turn. Lucy would have to seek the help of her daughters as her advancing age and declining health took a toll on her well being.

Lucille Walker and children 75th birthday

Chapter Twenty One

Death of a Soldier's Wife

Katie Lucille (Lucy) Walker was a soldier's wife. She had great internal strength and fortitude. Her outlook on life was extremely positive. She weathered the storms of life and bounced back with vigor that few men or women would ever possess. However, she was a woman of unwavering compassion to be the best at all she attempted. Her Christian life was no different. Her strict moral upbringing had gotten her through struggles and trials without losing faith in her God and her eternal home.

Lucy had grown up in the cotton fields of North Alabama as the daughter of poor subsistence farmers. She had faced dire situations with the possibility that she might lose her young military husband if she did not consent to his leg being taken off at the groin. She had gone to foreign lands on her own with her young children. She had lost all her belongings on two occasions during military moves. Katie Lucille had survived deadly situations with grace and courage. She faced down threats to her life and family from two world superpowers in Berlin, Germany, and Tripoli, Libya.

While serving as a soldier's wife, Katie Lucille Walker had lost two of her babies. She lost her loving mother Maudy Nevady (Vady) Walker when she was in Italy thousands of miles away from her childhood home. Lucy suffered untold and unbearable grief because she did not get to attend her mother's funeral, but again she bounced back as strong as ever.

Within some two years of her mother's death, Lucy lost her father at the time her husband was serving two years in Vietnam. She was in Texas when she got the feared knock on the door and received the news that her father, Reverend Monroe Daniel (Dan) Walker, had died. It appeared that she had inherited her great emotional strength and power from her father. She, like her dad, had a Christian faith that was unmovable and founded upon the rock; the rages of life would never shake the foundation of the soldier's wife.

Lucy had to give up being with her husband for over two years while he served his country in the Vietnam War; eventually, she lost her soldier, Asa (Ace) Francis Walker, Jr. She lost two of her beloved grandchildren. She had lost all her brothers and sisters, but still she weathered the storms of life and survived the great waves of heavy grief and deep sorrow. However, these forces were taking their toll on Katie Lucille (Lucy) Walker.

Katie Lucille always emerged on the other side of all the worldly forces with a smile on her face and the love of God in her heart, but there was one last battle in the war of life that she could not conquer. This time she would not bounce back, but she would join her loved ones who had already lost their battle for life.

Her health was declining, but few people were aware of her condition. Aunt Lucille rarely complained. She developed a type of kidney failure which was speculated to be caused by a severe wreck that she had barely survived. About two years after the crash, she developed severe itching on the bottom of her feet, palms of her hands, inside her ears, and other places.

After seeing a doctor Katie Lucille was told that she would have to start dialysis. For a few years, she refused treatments. Then, she experienced a very bad sickness episode because her kidneys were totally shutting down. The doctor told her that she would have less than forty eight hours to live unless her blood was cleansed. Reluctantly, Lucy agreed to start dialysis.

Martha Jo would take her mother to the dialysis clinic four times per week for four hours each session. By the time Martha Jo would get her home, Lucy would be too weak to walk, and she had to be carried in the house. After each session, Katie Lucille would vomit for about twenty four hours. She continued the treatments for three weeks and decided that she would not have any more treatments. Her doctors convinced Lucy to try home dialysis; Lucy, Jo, and Cynthia went through five days of dialysis training, after which Lucy began doing her dialysis at home three times per day. For the last eight years her life, Katie Lucille was dependent on home dialysis to cleanse her blood.

Always a strong and beautiful lady, Aunt Lucille was fighting a personal battle, but she was still a strong woman. The last few times I interviewed her, I sat in her home watching her do a two hour dialysis on her own. I was amazed at her positive attitude while she was attached to her dialysis equipment, but she had that smile on her face while she related life stories. Anyone who knew my Aunt Lucille would agree that she had a contagious laugh, warm caring eyes, and a kind heart.

In October before she died in February, Aunt Lucille nicked her leg on the car door. The wound would not heal and after several weeks with a constant fever, Jo contacted the doctor's office because Lucy refused to go to the doctor. During my last interview, she had her infected leg elevated, but still she was willing to pour out her life's story with that unending smile. She wanted this book to be written so that after her death her descendants would know her as a soldier's wife.

After that final interview, the doctor applied a wet bandage cast on her leg, but while doing so pinched another spot that formed a sore. After removing the bandaged, the doctors determined that she had no blood flow in her leg veins. They told her of drastic measures that must be taken to save her life.

With her leg not healing and very badly inflamed, the doctors eventually did a vein transplant which also failed. Katie Lucille was told by her doctors that they must remove her leg because sepsis had caused a life threatening complication of the infection. Sepsis released chemicals into Lucy's bloodstream which would eventually trigger inflammatory responses throughout her body that could cause multiple organ failure and death unless her leg was removed quickly.

I am sure Aunt Lucille considered the decision she had made not to have her young husband's leg removed when he had a skiing accident in Alaska that had broken his leg in thirteen places. She had not taken the doctor's advice to remove his leg; however, Asa was young and strong enough to overcome the severe physical damage. Now in order to save her own life, Lucy had to decide for herself if she would allow the doctors to remove her leg above her knee; the choice would be hers to make.

Again Katie Lucille had to make a life or death decision, but this time it was her life hanging in the balance. I think everyone knew the decision that she would and did make. Without any show of fear, Lucy would not consent to having her leg removed, but she did not have youthful vigor on her side. She told the two doctors who came to her hospital room early one morning to prepare her for surgery that she loved them both, but that she wanted her daughters to carry her home to die.

Instead of surgery, Martha Jo and Cynthia carried their mother home. Lucy was at her home by nine o'clock that same morning. Sepsis quickly ravaged her body, and within a few days, life for Katie Lucille Walker would all be over. But, before she died, Lucy talked to each one of her children, just one on one. She told each child that she loved them, and she wanted them to go to church.

On my last visit while she was still alive, Aunt Lucille was bedfast, her eyes were closed, there was not the usual smile on her face, her breathing was heavily labored, and God was waiting to take her into his arms. Just a few hours later on February 28, 2014, my Aunt Katie Lucille (Lucy) Walker finished her eighty year course of life on earth. The soldier's wife followed her military husband and loved ones who had gone before into eternity.

Both Asa (Ace) Francis Walker, Jr. and Katie Lucille (Lucy) Walker are buried in the Friendship Baptist Cemetery at Upshaw in Winston County, Alabama. Asa's faithful wife was buried next to him on March 2, 2014, after her death on February 28, 2014. Lucy is buried where her parents Dan and Vady Walker and other kinfolks were interned.

Lucy's life was black and white. You always knew where she stood. Her stand was upon that rock of life that she was shown during her childhood. Even though her early days in the cotton fields were rough, her parents had taught Lucy to stand upon a solid Christian foundation which she did to her last days on earth. She was a strong woman and the epitome of what it took to be a soldier's wife.

Katie Lucille Walker supported her husband during his career in the military without ever knowing the details of his activities. Lucy had always lived in the gray areas of her husband's military duties because of his top secret security clearance. She never had a clear understanding of all the things her husband was involved with during his time in the military.

Because of his top secret security clearance, Asa Francis Walker, Jr. could not discuss his military obligations, the covert experiences, or underground duties that he was involved with during the Cold War. From the end of World War II, the Korean War, and the Vietnam War, Asa Walker served the United States with honor and respect. His loyalty to wife, children, family, and country went beyond mere words.

Katie Lucille (Lucy) Walker and Asa Francis Walker, Jr.

As a soldier in the United States military, Asa had dedicated his life to serve our nation, and Lucy was his biggest supporter. Many times his soldier's wife from the cotton fields of Alabama had no idea of the dangers Asa faced during his twenty four years in the security service. But for his last twelve years, Asa was the biggest supporter of Katie Lucille in her successful Avon career which spanned some twenty six years.

On February 28, 2014, Katie Lucille (Lucy) Walker took to her death many of the trials and tribulations that she had overcome during Asa Francis Walker's military career and later. Husband and wife had worked to the benefit of each other from the day they said, "I do" until death where they were united again in eternity. Asa and Lucy were interned side by side never to be separated again. Asa was a soldier! Katie Lucille was a soldier's wife!

I interviewed my Aunt Lucille many times prior to her death as I worked on two of my books: Celtic Indian Boy of Appalachia; and, Soldier's Wife, the book about her life following her military husband. But as I wrote on her book after she died, I had a thousand questions I wanted to ask. Many wonderful experiences and stories of a personal nature, she took to the grave. I encourage everyone to talk to your elders before it is too late. Record your family stories while there is still time to talk to your parents and grandparents.

Soldier's Wife is dedicated to my wonderful and loving Aunt Katie Lucille (Lucy) Walker and her children, Martha Jo, Mark, Asa Lynn, Cynthia, and Roger. With a big smile on her face, Aunt Lucille always had a kind word to say to me. I was honored to write the story of her life.

"Soldier's Wife"

IN MEMORY
Of
Katie Lucille (Lucy) Walker

May 26, 1933-February 28, 2014

Chapter Twenty Two

Memorials for a Soldier's Wife

Soon upon her return to Alabama in 1972, Katie Lucille (Lucy) Walker started going to church with her older sisters Lodean Walker Prater and Violene Walker Welborn Killen. Lodean's daughter Sylvia had married Francis Proctor who was a preacher and leader of a local church that was known as Speake Christian Fellowship. Lucy joined the church and actively attended all services. She became a dedicated member of the church.

Martha Jo Walker Wise said, "When mother joined Speake Christian Fellowship, she made an outward change. She quit wearing makeup and dressed very conservatively."

Aunt Lucille wanted to make sure people knew that she had an inward change that she reflected with an outward appearance. Even though she had always been a Christian lady, she wanted to convey an outward expression of her walk with God. She did just that!

Since her sisters attended the church that was just a few miles northwest from her home on Highway 157, Lucy's became an active member and developed a deeper Christian faith as she got older. She had grown up in a very devout Baptist home where Bible reading by her father Dan Walker was a daily activity. Martha Jo Walker Wise told me, "Since 1972 while she was attending Speake Christian Fellowship, my mother spent twenty to twenty five hours per week working or worshipping in her church."

I gave all the children of Katie Lucille Walker an opportunity to tell what their mother meant to them. In addition, other people wrote statements about the strong Christian woman that meant so much to their lives. My Aunt Katie Lucille (Lucy) Walker was an inspiration to the many folks that knew her. She made a difference in so many lives. She dedicated her life to serving God, family and country.

Martha Jo Walker Wise-tribute to her mom

Martha Jo was born on April 2, 1954, at Fort George G. Meade, Maryland. She was the oldest child of Katie Lucille (Lucy) Walker. As a youngster, Jo depended on her mother for support in all that she attempted and accomplished. Lucy provided her daughter with a solid foundation by being the strong woman role model of a soldier's wife. However, as they got older, the roles were reversed with Lucy depending on Martha Jo for assistance and guidance.

Lucy and Jo

Martha Jo was always there for her mother and stood by her mom in sickness and in health. Jo was Lucy's best Avon supporter, employee, and partner, but Jo was also her primary caretaker. For Avon deliveries, trainings, seminars, meetings, luncheons, and trips, Jo was there to back up her mother.

182

Through all the pain, sickness, dialysis, appointments, doctor visits, and hospital stays, Jo was always there for her mother. Mother and daughter inspired each other as the time clock of life got closer to striking the final hours for Lucy. The words and statements of Martha Jo tell how she felt about her mother.

"My mom Katie Lucille (Lucy) Walker"

"My mom was to most people:

Strong
Faithful
Compassionate
Loving
Serving
Realistic
Beautiful
Funny
Honest
Determined

My mom to me as a child:

My nurse for hurt fingers
My cook for new foods
My guide to the world
My teacher for packing quickly
My hand to hold when it was dark
My enemy when she said NO
My only constant when we moved
Family is all that you will ever have
Taught me possessions are only things
Taught me friends are for leaving
Told me to always wear clean underwear
The military is always right
Always be good; daddy will get in trouble
Keep all affairs in order; you might have to leave tomorrow

My mom was to me as an adult:

My opponent in rook or spades
My partner in business
My mentor in life
My other half in scrabble
My worst enemy in some of my wants
My best friend most of the time
My boss in business
My helpmate in decision making
My go to on the bible
My prayer partner
My shoulder to cry on
My idea bouncer offer
My loan officer
My babysitter
Always smelled like Wings

My mom taught me:

Read the bible for strength for today
Always pray before you decide to do something
Do what you say you will do; be dependable
A little lie is still a lie
Words DO hurt; watch what you say
Always say you are doing good; no matter what
To strive to be the best you can be
If you never ask, the answer is always NO
If you reach for the moon, you might fall among the stars

My wish is:

That I could have as many people think as highly of me as they did my mom.
That I could have her determination and drive, but there is only one that had all
that, and that was **My MOM"**

Mark Steven Walker-message from his family

Mark Steven Walker was born on July 9, 1955, in Hartselle, Alabama. He was the second child and oldest son of Katie Lucille (Lucy) Walker. Mark was the only baby to be born in Morgan County, Alabama, where his parents had lived prior to their life in the military. Mark was born at the Hartselle Hospital in the same town that his father called home. He made the following statement concerning his mother.

"My family and I miss her dearly! She will always have a Special place in our hearts!"

Asa Lynn Walker-Unspeakable Love

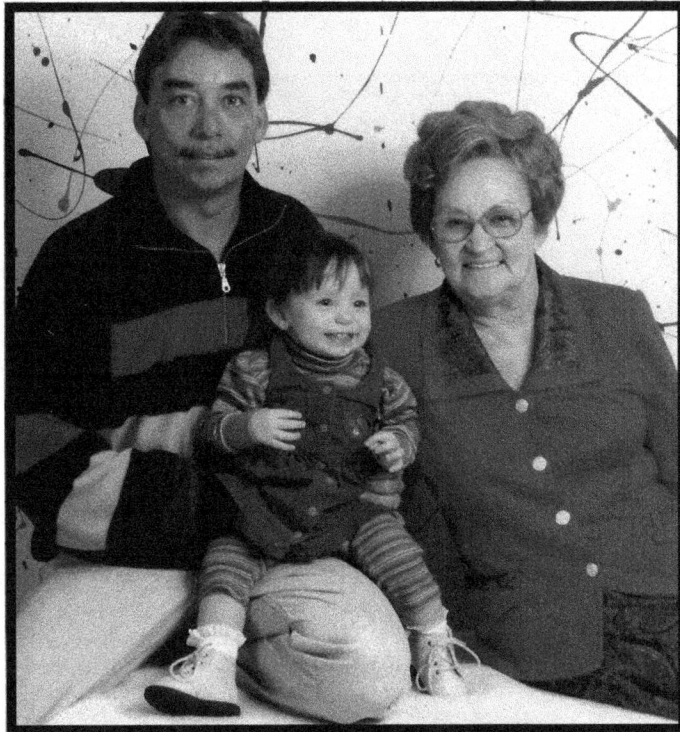

Asa Lynn, Lila, and Lucy

Asa Lynn Walker was born on April 6, 1957, at Maxwell Air Force Base in Montgomery, Alabama. He was the third child and second son of Katie Lucille (Lucy) Walker. Asa Lynn said:

"I have a personality and nature more like my mother than that of my father. I loved my mother to the bottom of my heart, and I have a very difficult time talking about her."

Cynthia Sue Walker Curatola-loving note about her momma

Cynthia Sue Walker Curatola was born on January 2, 1966, at Fort George G. Meade, Maryland. She was the fourth child and second daughter of Katie Lucille (Lucy) Walker. According to her older sister, Cynthia was not a planned child. A year before she was born, Lucy had lost her second child by miscarriage and decided not to have any more children. Cynthia's older sister Martha Jo Walker Wise said that Cynthia was an "oops," but she was a blessing to parents. Cynthia was extremely close to her mother. Cynthia wrote the following about her mother.

Lucy and Cynthia

"Momma was the glue that held the family together. Her strength and tenacity was nothing short of amazing grace-God breathed. She walked not in the counsel of the wicked, or stood in the way of the scornful, nor set with mockers. She was a tree planted beside the still waters and yielded all kind of fruit in her season.

My momma meditated on God's Word. She was the best Jesus I ever came in contact with. On my worse day, she always encouraged me and told me that I was beautiful. She was my heart, my best-friend, my confident, and my biggest cheerleader. When everybody else kicked me while I was down, my Momma never quit, never gave up, always believed in me, and was always there for me. I miss her more than words can say..."

Roger Walker-I loved my MOMMA

Roger Walker was born on June 6, 1967, in the war torn City of Tripoli, Libya. He was the fifth child and third son of Katie Lucille (Lucy) Walker. He was induced to be born during the revolution led by Colonel Muammar Gaddafi. Roger was too young to remember the military style of life lived by his mother and father. Unlike his three oldest siblings, he grew up in one place. Roger developed roots with school friends. He had a stable childhood with very few moves. Roger lived next door to his mother and depended on her probably more than his other siblings; seeing his mother was a daily ritual. No doubt that Roger had a deep love for his mother. She was one of the most special women in his life. He made only four statements about his momma, but those remarks came deep from within his heart.

Lucy and Roger

"Mom made my life more meaningful!
Mom was my best friend!
Mom was always there for me!
She was my MOMMA!"

Lila Walker-eulogy to her grandmother

Lila Walker is the daughter of Asa Lynn Walker and granddaughter of Katie Lucille (Lucy) Walker. Lila graduated from Lawrence County High School in Moulton, Alabama. Presently, she is attending the University of North Alabama. Lila wrote the following about her grandmother.

"My grandmother had to be the most positive person that I have ever known. I am not exaggerating when I say I have never heard a complaint come out of her mouth; even when she honestly deserved it. All that came out of her mouth was love and positivity.

Even before she passed away, we all knew she was in tons of pain, and she would be asleep for days. When she rarely woke up, she would utter "God is good." And I would feel so awful and unjustified for all my petty complaints and negative words because here my sick granny is, complaining none, but testifying God's goodness. She invested in it, she read her Bible everyday more than once, she prayed all the time, and rather than bashing what she hated, she promoted what she loved."

Sylvia Prater Proctor-description of her special aunt

The following testimony was given by Sylvia Prater Proctor who is the niece of Katie Lucille Walker. She was the daughter of Katie Lucille Walker's sister Lodean Walker who had married Lucian Prater. Sylvia and Aunt Lucille went to church together for several years. She explained what her aunt meant to her.

Sylvia said, "I do not have the words to describe a woman that is so very special to me. Aunt Lucille was always an aunt that I could count on. She was always someone in my life that I knew would go the extra mile to do something to help others. As I grew up, I watched her continually give both in word and deed.

When Francis and I became the pastor of Speake Christian Fellowship, Aunt Lucille went with us. She was the most faithful member. When we needed someone to teach a children's Sunday school class, Aunt Lucille would say, 'I will do it'; adult Sunday school class…. 'I will do it.'

When we had yard sales and chicken stew fund raisers, Aunt Lucille was always there to help. For special dinners, luncheons, gatherings, you could always count on Aunt

Slyvia Proctor and Lucille Walker

189

Lucille to bring the just right dish.

As our ministry grew at Speake Christian Fellowship, she grew right along with us. When we dedicated time and financial resources to ministry and missionaries, Aunt Lucille said, 'How can I help?' Missionaries from across the world have been touched by the kindness and giving spirit of her love for Christ.

Aunt Lucille became my right hand prayer partner and warrior. I knew that I could call her at any time of the day or night, and she would join with me in prayer believing for God's blessings and answers to our prayers. She demonstrated a true servant's heart each and every day. She was always thinking of others, giving of herself, wearing a beautiful smile, and speaking kind words to all that she came in contact with. Aunt Lucille was the most giving aunt in the world. I think of her every day."

Martha Lawrence-Christian friend of Katie Lucille Walker

Martha Lawrence wrote a memorial to Katie Lucille (Lucy) Walker as her dear friend. Lucy was her Avon sales lady and her worship partner. The following is a statement from Ms. Martha Lawrence about her Christian friend.

"Lucy Walker was a true friend and a great Christian lady. She was a Sunday school teacher for the adult ladies and men's class for a few years. She then became the secretary and treasurer for about eighteen to twenty years.

In November 1995, I was going through a very bad time in my life. At the time, my son was going through a divorce. During this stressful period, I was attending another church that was also going through some turbulent situations. The pastor of the church came to me and said, 'Sister if you are looking for a more spirit filled church, then you may need to look for somewhere else to attend worship.'

The preacher told me that on a Sunday, and on that following Tuesday, Ms. Lucy Walker came by my house with her Avon products. We talked and I told her some of the problems I was facing. After hearing my story, she invited me to go to church with her. Lucy was not just another Avon lady; it was a working of God that was calling me through my dear friend.

Ms. Lucy was attending Speake Christian Fellowship. We talked about all the good things of God that was happening at her church. The next Sunday, I went to church with Ms. Lucy. I still attend church at Speake Christian Fellowship, today.

In December of 2014, I was asked to take over the secretary of the ladies class at the church. Before Ms. Lucy got so sick, she had a neat little book and a small bag with the money. I still have all the stuff that Ms. Lucy used. It passed on to me after she died.

I miss Sister Lucy more and more every day. She believed in prayer and then let the Lord take care of the rest. Ms. Lucy was a true, loving, caring friend. I miss her dearly."

Katie Lucille Walker was dedicated to her church

Barbara (Bob) Crow-Aunt Lucy

Barbara (Bob) Crow was an Avon customer of Katie Lucille (Lucy) Walker. She is also a dear friend of mine, and she talked highly of my Aunt Lucille Waker.

Bob Crow said, "Aunt Lucy Walker, what a remarkable lady she was! The peace and tranquility she exuded, even knowing she was facing eminent death, was inspirational indeed. The amazing experiences she survived during her lifetime one might expect would cause a bitterness or resentment, not so for Aunt Lucy!

Her bright eyes and sweet, precious smile when you entered her presence made you feel as though you'd been given a big hug! She was this lovely, peaceful, and wonderful lady who never gave a clue to the health problems she was experiencing or the sometimes terrifying and painful episodes in her life as a young military wife and mother.

I feel blessed to have known her for a much too limited time. I know her family misses her terribly. I am grateful to my friend Rickey Butch Walker for recording her remarkable experiences which enables us to know truly how rare a person Aunt Lucy Walker was. This tribute to Aunt Lucy Walker will not soon be forgotten as you journey through these pages with her into a very surprising life!"

Index

195

Books by Rickey Butch Walker

Doublehead Last Chickamauga Cherokee Chief
ISBN # 978-1-934610-67-1

http://amzn.to/1wSCjXt

Chickasaw Chief George Colbert: His Family and His Country

ISBN # 978-1-934610-71-8

http://amzn.to/1wSDKFo

Warrior Mountains Folklore

ISBN # 978-1-934610-65-7

http://amzn.to/1zsXsf7

Celtic Indian Boy of the Appalachia: A Scots Irish Cherokee Childhood

ISBN # 978-1-934610-75-6

http://amzn.to/1z1ufEr

Appalachian Indian Trails of the Chickamauga: Lower Cherokee Settlements

ISBN # 978-1-934610-91-6

http://amzn.to/16hpHE4

Hiking Sipsey: A Family's Fight for Eastern Wilderness

ISBN # 978-1-934610-91-6

http://amzn.to/1CnPKqi

Appalachian Indians of the Warrior Mountains

ISBN # 978-1-934610-72-5

http://amzn.to/1EYbwPL

Warrior Mountains Indian Heritage - Teacher's Edition

ISBN # 978-1-934610-27-5

http://amzn.to/168WBWh

Warrior Mountains Indian Heritage Student Edition

ISBN # 978-1-934610-66-4

http://amzn.to/1EyUavd

Other Southeastern Native American Publications

Speech of an Indian

ISBN # 978-1-934610-97-8

By Robert Perry

http://amzn.to/1ldnWWq

Three Tribes of Little People

ISBN # 978-1-934610-95-4

By Robert Perry

http://amzn.to/1OfRpiH

Bluewater Publications is a multi-faceted publishing company capable of meeting all of your reading and publishing needs. Our two-fold aim is to:

1) Provide the market with educationally enlightening and inspiring research and reading materials.

2) Make the opportunity of being published available to any author and or researcher who desire to be published.

We are passionate about preserving history; whether through the re-publishing of an out-of-print classic, or by publishing the research of historians and genealogists. Bluewater Publications is the *Peoples' Choice Publisher*.

For company information or information about how you can be published through Bluewater Publications, please visit:

www.BluewaterPublications.com

Also check Amazon.com to purchase any of the books that we publish.

Confidently Preserving Our Past,

Bluewater Publications.com

www.ingramcontent.com/pod-product-compliance
Lightning Source LLC
Chambersburg PA
CBHW050459110426
42742CB00018B/3313